Campus Crime: Compliance And Enforcement Under The Clery Act

United States Congress Senate Committee on Judiciary

S. Hrg. 109–590

CAMPUS CRIME: COMPLIANCE AND ENFORCEMENT UNDER THE CLERY ACT

HEARING

BEFORE THE

COMMITTEE ON THE JUDICIARY
UNITED STATES SENATE

ONE HUNDRED NINTH CONGRESS

SECOND SESSION

MAY 19, 2006

PHILADELPHIA, PENNSYLVANIA

Serial No. J–109–79

Printed for the use of the Committee on the Judiciary

U.S. GOVERNMENT PRINTING OFFICE

30–043 PDF   WASHINGTON : 2006

For sale by the Superintendent of Documents, U.S. Government Printing Office
Internet: bookstore.gpo.gov   Phone: toll free (866) 512–1800; DC area (202) 512–1800
Fax: (202) 512–2250   Mail: Stop SSOP, Washington, DC 20402–0001

COMMITTEE ON THE JUDICIARY

ARLEN SPECTER, Pennsylvania, *Chairman*

ORRIN G. HATCH, Utah
CHARLES E. GRASSLEY, Iowa
JON KYL, Arizona
MIKE DeWINE, Ohio
JEFF SESSIONS, Alabama
LINDSEY O. GRAHAM, South Carolina
JOHN CORNYN, Texas
SAM BROWNBACK, Kansas
TOM COBURN, Oklahoma

PATRICK J. LEAHY, Vermont
EDWARD M. KENNEDY, Massachusetts
JOSEPH R. BIDEN, JR., Delaware
HERBERT KOHL, Wisconsin
DIANNE FEINSTEIN, California
RUSSELL D. FEINGOLD, Wisconsin
CHARLES E. SCHUMER, New York
RICHARD J. DURBIN, Illinois

MICHAEL O'NEILL, *Chief Counsel and Staff Director*
BRUCE A. COHEN, *Democratic Chief Counsel and Staff Director*

CONTENTS

STATEMENT OF COMMITTEE MEMBER

WITNESSES

SUBMISSIONS FOR THE RECORD

CAMPUS CRIME: COMPLIANCE AND ENFORCEMENT UNDER THE CLERY ACT

FRIDAY, MAY 19, 2006

U.S. SENATE,
COMMITTEE ON THE JUDICIARY,
Washington, DC.

The Committee met, pursuant to notice, at 2:06 p.m., at the National Constitution Center, Philadelphia, Pennsylvania, Hon. Arlen Specter, Chairman of the Committee, presiding.

Present: Senators Specter, Santorum.

OPENING STATEMENT OF HON. ARLEN SPECTER, A U.S. SENATOR FROM THE STATE OF PENNSYLVANIA

Chairman SPECTER. Good afternoon, ladies and gentlemen. We will now proceed with an oversight hearing under the auspices of the Senate Judiciary Committee and under the auspices of the Senate Appropriation Subcommittee on Labor, Health, Human Services and Education.

We are going to be examining today the enforcement of the Clery Act, an act named for Jeanne Clery, who was a 19-year-old freshman at Lehigh University back in 1986 when she was the victim of a brutal rape and murder. Her parents came to me at that time, and the Clery family has, in the intervening years, become crusaders for campus safety. As a result of their initiative, we enacted legislation which requires universities and colleges to report what is happening on the campuses with respect to violence and criminal activity.

The enforcement has been under the Department of Education, and it appears, and this is subject to our oversight inquiry, that the Department of Education has not done an adequate job of enforcing the statute.

I'm advised that since the statute was enacted, which was 20 years ago, there have only been three enforcement proceedings at which fines were levied. We'll be asking Mr. Baker, who's the representative of the Department of Education, about that here later this afternoon.

There was an extensive story in the Philadelphia Inquirer back in January which particularized what's happening on local campuses, and the picture was not good. The picture was very bad. The local universities had been reporting very little in the way of crime statistics, and then once the Inquirer started to investigate, stir it up, suddenly reports were modified and amended.

This is a very, very important statute, because if you do not know what is happening on the campus, parents cannot make an

(1)

evaluation as to where they want to send their children to school. And if you don't report what is happening on the campus, students and parents are not able to protect themselves. And if you don't report what is happening on the campus, then the campus officials are not alerted to the need to provide some local policing, and the local law enforcement officials and the local police are not on notice. So we're not kidding when we say this reporting is important. And it's not been done.

Senator Santorum and I have been discussing this situation and we want to find out what the facts are. But based on what we see on the record, we would have to move from the Department of Education to the Department of Justice. The Department of Justice is in the business of enforcing the law, but so is the Department of Education. We may have to move away from just fines to criminal jail sanctions.

There's a rising debate as to the extent to which tougher statutes should deter street crime, but there's no debate about criminal penalties and jail deterring white collar crime. I'll be looking for confirmation of that by U.S. Attorney Pat Meehan in a few minutes, but I was a district attorney for quite a while and I know the impact of jail sentences on white collar crime.

We have some of the leading professionals in this audience today from the universities, and the universities in this community and America at large do a great job. They do the impossible job. They've educated Rick and me.

[Laughter.]

Chairman SPECTER. We're a big university town and I'm very proud of what goes on in this city and what goes on in this State and what goes on in the country. And the university administrators want to do the right thing, but there's going to have to be a different degree of vigilance if we're to see that this Act is enforced.

Let me yield now to my distinguished colleague, Senator Santorum.

STATEMENT OF HON. RICK SANTORUM, A U.S. SENATOR FROM THE STATE OF PENNSYLVANIA

Senator SANTORUM. Thank you, Senator Specter. I just want to thank you first for the work that you've done in the past on this legislation. As the author of the Clery Act, you should take great pride in the amount of comfort that you've given to many parents and children as they search for the college they want to attend and get the relevant information that they need to be able to make that decision. Through your work, through your continued diligence in making sure that the Act is complied with, you have provided a lot of help to a lot of parents and a lot of kids.

As the father of two teenagers, one of whom will be a sophomore in high school this year, we're just beginning to take a look at what colleges and universities that may be on her agenda. I will tell you, as a parent, I certainly want to know that information, and I want to know that that information is accurate. I think that's the least that we can provide, that if we have a statute on the books that is there to inform parents and kids as to what the crime statistics are, that the statute is being enforced and the information that they are being given can be relied upon. Otherwise, ill-informed decisions are made, and sometimes that can lead to bad consequences.

I congratulate you, Senator, for the work you're doing, I congratulate you for this hearing. I want to say that I do also have concerns about whether the Department, given its record of enforcement, is, No. 1, committed to enforcement; and, No. 2, is capable of adequate enforcement.

Hopefully, this hearing today will shed some light on both of those things, their level of commitment and their ability to be able to do this job and do it effectively, and whether there are alternatives, as Senator Specter suggested we could look at, whether this needs to migrate over to an agency that is more in line with uncovering criminal activity, and that would be the Justice Department.

Second, I think, Senator, you mentioned the other issue here, which is the fact that the Department has not fined any of these colleges and universities. We see from ample evidence on the record that many colleges and universities have failed to comply with the Act, yet very few have been fined.

I'm not a big guy going around that we need departments in government running around fining everybody at the drop of the hat. I very much believe in a regulatory environment that encourages compliance and that is not driven by penalties.

But when we see that there is not compliance and that problem seems to be a persistent problem, and then we see no penalties on top of it, then I'm wondering whether you have neither a compliance or a criminal approach to the problem, and that is just candidly not acceptable.

Final point Senator Specter made, which is the nature of the enforcement, whether fines are sufficient. I certainly would hesitate to increase those penalties to include prison time, but I'm hopeful that we can stop short of that and that we can see a better record of compliance.

Let me just suggest that if that is not forthcoming, that those are options that certainly have to be discussed and laid on the table.

Again, Mr. Chairman, you've been a busy man this last week or two. In fact, you've been a busy man this year on a whole lot of issues. For you to take the time to focus on this I think just shows your commitment to this issue, and you're to be congratulated for your determination in making sure that this law is adequately enforced.

Chairman SPECTER. Thank you very much, Senator Santorum. Thank you for your participation and thank you for the outstanding job you're doing in the U.S. Senate for the 12 million people in Pennsylvania.

I want to acknowledge the presence today of Mrs. Connie Clery, Jeanne Clery's mother, who has been a real crusader on this issue, and also Mr. Benjamin Clery, brother of Jeanne Clery, who is president of Security On Campus.

We turn now to our first witness, who is Mr. Robert Baker, the Region III representative for the U.S. Secretary of Education. I'd hoped the Secretary could have been here, but she's in Europe at the present time. We have a little bit of sway on her scheduling since we appropriate $52 billion a year for her department in the Subcommittee which I chair.

Mr. Baker has his BA degree from University of Pennsylvania, 1973; he has served as deputy secretary of the Department of Labor and Industry of Pennsylvania; deputy secretary of the Pennsylvania Department of Commerce. He will put a more expansive statement in the record.

We have 5 minutes for each witness, and the floor is yours, Mr. Baker.

STATEMENT OF ROBERT BAKER, REGION III REPRESENTATIVE FOR SECRETARY OF EDUCATION MARGARET SPELLINGS, DEPARTMENT OF EDUCATION, WASHINGTON, D.C.

Mr. BAKER. Thank you, Mr. Chairman, Senator Santorum, thank you for providing me the opportunity to appear before you today to talk about the U.S. Department of Education's implementation of the Jeanne Clery Disclosure of Campus Security Policy and Campus Crime Statistics Act.

Crime on college campuses is a priority on parents' minds as their children leave home to attend college. As a parent of a son who is attending West Chester University and will be transferring to the School of Engineering at Temple this fall, I am deeply concerned about campus security.

When we send our children off to college, we expect the college or university to ensure that they're learning in a safe environment, free of concern from crime. Practically, we realize that no school, just like no community, is crime free, and as parents we must make an informed decision whether or not a certain school might expose our child to undue risk. The reporting requirements of the Clery Act provide important resources to parents and students to help them make that determination.

The Department's committed to assisting institutions of higher education in providing the students nationwide a safe environment in which to learn and to keep students, parents, and employees well informed about campus security.

To help institutions comply with the requirements of the Clery Act, the Department, at the direction and urging of Congress, published The Handbook for Campus Crime Reporting in June 2005. The handbook was developed in response to the needs expressed by the community for more detailed and complete guidance on Clery Act implementation.

The Department has provided training for institutions, campus security administrators, law enforcement, law enforcement associations, and Department staff. Since 2002, approximately 1,000 individuals have participated in our training activities. The Department also plans to provide additional training to Department staff in all aspects of the Clery Act in October of this year.

We have achieved great success in our data collection. With the exception of institutions that were affected by Hurricanes Katrina and Rita last year, we have had a 100 percent response rate in each of the past 6 years. We are proud of this response rate and believe that it demonstrates a commitment by institutions to comply with the spirit of the Clery Act. It also demonstrates the strength of the Department's determination to ensure compliance with the Act.

Campus safety is a collaborative effort among various components of institutions of higher education and local law enforcement. On occasion collaboration also extends to the Federal level to the Department of Education, the U.S. Attorney's Office, and the Federal Bureau of Investigation. In addition, it would be difficult to accomplish our implementation and enforcement efforts without the assistance of groups such as Security On Campus and the International Association of Campus Law Enforcement Administrators.

The Department suggests ongoing monitoring of institutions of post secondary education that participate in the Federal student aid programs. We look at compliance with Clery Act requirements as a part of each and every program review we conduct.

The Department also conducts focused campus security program reviews to determine whether an institution is in compliance with the Clery Act.

Between 1994 and 2006, the Department conducted 4,623 program reviews, 17 of which were focused on campus security and compliance. Of the remaining 4,606 reviews, 252 of those identified violations of the Clery Act.

From time to time, through those targeted program reviews, we have found significant instances of non-compliance. In these cases we have imposed fines. In 2000 we imposed a $15,000 fine on Mount St. Clare College. In April of 2005, a fine of $200,000 was imposed on Salem International University. Most recently, in October 2005 the Department fined Miami University of Ohio $27,500. We impose fines only when absolutely necessary to ensure continuing compliance with the requirements of the Clery Act and when evidence points to substantial misrepresentation.

Presently we have pending 26 program reviews that became violations of Clery Act requirements. Additional fines are possible in these cases when final determinations are issued.

Earlier I mentioned the cooperation of the FBI. I believe we need to expand that relationship to explore asking the Bureau to conduct audits of crime statistics at a sampling of schools across the country. The FBI already conducts audits of local law enforcement agencies and is skilled at identifying proper crime reporting. Working together, we could gain an even better understanding of compliance of the Clery Act, and reinforce the schools the importance of providing full and accurate information.

The fundamental premise of the Clery Act is having timely and accurate information about the frequency of crimes on college campuses that will enable parents, students, and prospective students to make good decisions about where to enroll in college and where to live at school. Having complete, accurate, and timely information regarding campus security is critical as students make these important choices and pay attention to their surroundings and their decisions regarding personal safety.

As a parent, I applaud the Clery family, Congress, and especially you, Mr. Chairman, for requiring post secondary schools to report this information that has proven invaluable to parents and students across the country.

I also want to thank you for holding this hearing today on this critical issue, and look forward to answering any questions you might have for the Department.

[The prepared statement of Mr. Baker appears as a submission for the record.]

Chairman SPECTER. Thank you very much, Mr. Baker.

We now turn to the United States Attorney for the Eastern District of Pennsylvania, Patrick Meehan. Mr. Meehan has a bachelor's degree from Bowdoin College, 1978; law degree from Temple; served as district attorney of Delaware County; he was an associate with the law firm of Dilworth Paxon; senior counsel and executive director of the Office of Arlen Specter, Philadelphia; also campaign manager for Arlen Specter, 1992, successful; campaign manager for Senator Santorum in 1994, successful.

Mr. Meehan, you're way ahead of the game so far. The next 5 minutes are yours.

STATEMENT OF PATRICK MEEHAN, U.S. ATTORNEY FOR THE EASTERN DISTRICT OF PENNSYLVANIA, DEPARTMENT OF JUSTICE, WASHINGTON, D.C.

Mr. MEEHAN. Thank you, Senator.

Mr. Chairman, Senator Santorum, thank you for the opportunity to testify about a matter that's of such concern to all of us. I know I've given substantial written comments, so let me take my limited opportunity to focus on an issue of significant importance to me.

I want to emphasize that the Clery Act asks for more than just reporting crimes and statistics. It requires schools to take steps to help prevent crime, but it also, of greatest importance, it requires schools to inform students about programs and services to protect and heal those students who, unfortunately, are victimized by crime, particularly sexual assault on campuses, which we find are often acquaintance assaults.

There have been recent reports in the press about problems of schools, particularly with regards to sexual assault. For example, at the University of Virginia, at Georgetown, at William and Mary, and Ohio State, five female students, one from each of these schools, reported to Dateline they were raped or forcibly assaulted sexually by fellow students.

The female students reported the alleged assaults to school officials, who allegedly either discouraged the victims from moving forward with their cases, or failed to take effective actions against the perpetrator. Student-on-student date rape have recurring themes on campuses across the country.

Congress, in fact, asked the National Institute of Justice to study school compliance with Federal laws regarding safety on campus, and particularly look at the issue of sexual assault on campus and what colleges and universities are doing about it.

In December of 2005, the NIJ published its findings, and the results of that study are sobering. The report itself states that sexual assault is widely considered to be the most underreported crime in America. It concluded that just under 3 percent of all college women become victims of rape during the 9 months of a typical school year. That's 35 crimes for every 1,000 women students on a campus.

Despite these troubling statistics, what they found is less than 5 percent of completed and attempted rapes are brought to the attention of campus authorities or law enforcement. So it's the students that are not bringing it to the attention of the university.

Therefore, the logical question becomes, what are schools doing and what can be done to encourage victims to come forward? What can be done to expand the victim's ability to proceed from being a victim to being a survivor, if one believes she's been sexually assaulted?

Under the Clery Act schools must develop and distribute a statement of policy and procedures students should follow if a sex offense occurs. Only about four in ten offer sexual assault training, and often that training is not for the general student population.

Schools must also inform students of their option to notify proper law enforcement authorities, including on-campus and local police, and the option to be assisted by campus authorities in notifying such authorities if a student so chooses. Fewer than half the schools studied inform students how to file criminal charges.

There are good stories. Lafayette College, for example, University of Pennsylvania here in Philadelphia have created model programs that allow a victim to participate in decisionmaking, have some control over the pace of the process and are in charge of making decisions. Some practices include identifying the specific person or office to contact when sexual assault has occurred; the option to confidential or maybe even anonymous reporting. The policies fully inform students of each of the separate actions available to the victim.

There are barriers, such as a failure of many people who are victims to recognize that that assault is a crime; there are concerns about confidentiality if they bring a report forward; and campus drug and alcohol policies, which may bring the victim into some kind of issue with the school itself, that works as a detriment to reporting.

So working with our client agency, the Department of Education, my office wants to encourage noncompliant schools to create effective compliance programs consistent with these model NIJ programs. We hope by working with the many universities with the Department of Education continuing to marshal our resources and expertise that we will be able to increase schools' compliance efforts and decrease the criminal conduct on campus, particularly crimes involving sexual assault.

Chairman SPECTER. Thank you very much, Mr. Meehan.

We now go to the round of questioning, 5 minutes for Senator Santorum and me.

I begin with you, Mr. Baker. Is it true that there have only been three fines imposed by the Department of Education since the Clery Act was passed in 1986?

Mr. BAKER. That's correct. I should point out that the way we determine fines is based on the severity of the violation.

Chairman SPECTER. Three fines imposed.

Mr. BAKER. That's correct.

Chairman SPECTER. Isn't that an incredibly small number, given the number of colleges and the amount of crime and the significant underreporting?

Mr. BAKER. Well, our goal is to try to get schools, obviously, to report correctly. And, of course, annually they're required to have an accounting firm or auditing firm look at all the information they provide us.

Chairman SPECTER. Let's deal with the three fines imposed in 20 years. How can there conceivably, possibly be a justification for such lax enforcement?

Mr. BAKER. Well, we believe that—what we're trying to work with the schools to get the reporting requirements correct. So we're looking really for—

Chairman SPECTER. You're trying to get the schools to comply. Congress passed a law to impose fines. Do you think we're kidding?

Mr. BAKER. Oh, no, not at all, sir.

Chairman SPECTER. Well, our mandate has been ignored, absolutely ignored with that kind of an enforcement record. You don't have to go behind that to make an analysis and see that there simply is no enforcement.

Mr. Meehan, the Department of Justice conducted a study in December 2005, entitled "Sexual Assault on Campuses: What the Colleges and Universities are Doing About It", and found that only a third of the institutions report their crime statistics in a way that is fully consistent with the Federal laws.

What can be done about it, in your opinion, to get compliance? Should we shift this to the Department of Justice?

I know you don't have enough cases to handle, so you have people sitting around. You're a very overburdened office, beyond any question.

But should Congress look to the Department of Justice, which has experience in law enforcement, to do this job?

Mr. MEEHAN. Well, Senator, I can say, to be sure, we look forward to working with our partners and—

Chairman SPECTER. Who's your partner, Mr. Meehan?

Mr. MEEHAN. The Department of Education is a client agency of mine.

Chairman SPECTER. Would you claim them as a partner when they've only imposed three fines in 20 years?

Mr. MEEHAN. We handle appellate issues.

Senator, I believe, in response to your question, that we can do more, and I want to be a participant in doing more.

The Department of Education has laid out a handbook that creates the reporting mechanisms that leave all doubt about ambiguity in the reporting requirements. This is available online. I know that this is only a 2005 report, but this should give any institution that wants to do it all of the information that they need to be compliant. When an institution is not compliant, armed with the facts, we would look forward to the opportunity to work with our partner.

Chairman SPECTER. Mr. Meehan, it isn't sufficient to say the report should give them notice, it isn't sufficient to say we should work with a partner.

In the context of noncompliance with fines, what would you think about imposing some stiffer penalties, some jail sentences for those who maliciously and willfully, on a repetitive basis, fail to report crimes?

There are plenty of statutes which you enforce which impose those kinds of jail sanctions for failure to report. What is your evaluation of the deterrent effect of those kinds of statutes on the books? How much more effective are those penalties and simple fines in getting people to comply without investigations and rigorous enforcement?

Mr. MEEHAN. Well, Senator, there's no doubt criminal sanction in any particular case gets the attention of somebody that may be on the receiving end of that sanction.

I will tell you by analogy we would also have very tremendous success in acquiring compliance with regulations and, in fact, performance. I will use an example, the tremendous work that we do in the healthcare field. For instance, nursing homes that do not meet their obligations to provide the quality—

Chairman SPECTER. Jail terms are possible?

Mr. MEEHAN. There can be jail terms.

Chairman SPECTER. And there's compliance with those statutes?

Mr. MEEHAN. More significantly, Senator, we have the opportunity to dramatically influence the funding that comes to those institutions. When we get the attention of those people, because we can use the full gamut of Federal resources to interrupt the funding, they begin to pay attention. But most significantly, it gives us the leverage then to work with the Department of Health and Human Services in that context. And we get relationships with them where they begin to put in the compliance programs that address the issues that we're looking for. That's why I spent time on my testimony talking about some of these best practices that can be aspired to, would make a significant difference if institutions aspire to them. If we could help get them to do some aspiration by virtue of some of our prosecution, I know speaking for myself as a U.S. attorney, I would be anxious to do that.

Chairman SPECTER. Thank you very much, Mr. Meehan. My time has expired so I yield now to my colleague, Senator Santorum.

Senator SANTORUM. I just want to continue on that line of questioning.

That handbook was issued in 2005?

Mr. BAKER. That's correct.

Senator SANTORUM. What was the guidance for the colleges and universities prior to the handbook being issued?

Mr. BAKER. The Federal student handbook was the guidance. As U.S. Attorney Meehan pointed out, it's not nearly as encompassing as the guidance we have now which, if you read it provides examples, illustrates—you can tell about how the law should be implemented.

So it's our goal to develop a guide which includes everything for folks from all the different communities we deal with, that we should have even greater compliance.

Senator SANTORUM. That handbook was issued when in 2005?

Mr. BAKER. I believe it was June of 2005, and we held training with our folks in November of 2005.

You should know that we also appear before various associations and various functions to provide instruction on how the program works, but in addition to that, Security On Campus is going to be holding its own training sessions using that handbook. We provided

2,000 of them to Security On Campus, and $25,000 to help them perform that training.

Senator SANTORUM. You said in your statement that you impose fines only when absolutely necessary. It seems to be a rather—obviously a high standard since only three fines have been imposed and I guess I have to give credit—in recent times there's been a great acceleration.

For the first 14 years there were no fines, so three in the last 6 years, at least there are some fines. So I maybe give credit for at least some fines being issued, but why such a standard as absolutely necessary for violations of this Act when the statute calls for fines when the Act is violated?

Mr. BAKER. Well, you brought up yourself, Senator, the fact that there was limited guidance, perhaps, before. The Federal student handbook was not as comprehensive as what we have. There were misunderstandings—

Senator SANTORUM. Let me ask you this. So you had an Act that the universities didn't understand, that the Department didn't provide clear guidance, and for close to 20 years that situation was maintained until—then you decide to issue a handbook?

Mr. BAKER. I think the guidance was clear enough. I'd like to say that we've made it much clearer.

Senator SANTORUM. If it was clear enough, then why wasn't there better enforcement? It's one or the other: It wasn't clear and it should have been enforced or it was clear and it wasn't enforced.

Mr. BAKER. I think there was adequate enforcement. We've had 252 violations that we identified through our program reviews. We've had another 17—

Senator SANTORUM. Stop right there. 252 program violations over the 20 years of the Act, is that it?

Mr. BAKER. Well, since 1994.

Senator SANTORUM. Since 1994. And of those, three have been fines. Any other actions taken other than fines?

Mr. BAKER. We've had—we worked with, obviously, each school to try to make sure that they take corrective action.

We talked earlier about the University of Pennsylvania, they were concerned whether they were meeting all the tenets of the Clery Act. We worked with them, and as a result they do provide an example of how it should be done to others across the country.

So it came as a positive result. We had no findings necessary in order to obtain that result. And that's what we generally find with schools we work with. They're willing to work with us and we help them identify or anything they've misidentified.

We also have a toll-free hotline they can call to help interpret the Act. It existed before, it exists today even under the new guidelines so they can make sure they get the classification correct.

Senator SANTORUM. Do you periodically go out and charge someone like the U.S. Attorney or the FBI to do an assessment as to whether the reporting is accurate? Is that something that you would do to determine whether there is compliance here?

Mr. MEEHAN. Well, Senator, it's not something that we would customarily do, although I can tell you as the United States Attorney I was very interested in issues within my own jurisdiction, particularly since this is an Act that relates to it. And when I assumed the position of U.S. Attorney I began to look at that.

I will tell you, we had very good cooperation. The Department of Education actually cooperated on investigations during my tenure, which raised my desire to work even more progressively with the Department of Education.

Senator SANTORUM. My question is: Does either you or your client do, routinely, check or hire someone or routinely check to see whether the reporting matches what someone believes? I mean, we have the article in the paper here recently that shows that there was a great discrepancy. Was that article incorrect? If it was incorrect, why? If it wasn't incorrect, why wasn't that caught by someone else before the newspaper caught it?

Mr. BAKER. Well, every year every school's Federal student aid program is monitored. It's independently audited by the independent firm. In that audit, included are the Clery statistics. So we have had 400 and some violations uncovered as a result of those independent audits.

In addition, we go out and do our own audits and we've done, as I said, some 4,623 program audits which have uncovered violations. We also have what we call campus security reviews where we think there may be a major issue and we will go in and do a very, very thorough investigation.

I should mention too again, as I mentioned in my testimony, we would welcome a discussion with the Federal Bureau of Investigation regarding—

Senator SANTORUM. I know I'm over time, I apologize, but you did audits, you have the schools that were listed in the paper. Do your audits support what was reported in the press or not? And if not, why not?

Mr. BAKER. Well, the activities that were reported in the press actually have not been—will not be included in the Clery report until at least 2005, which we won't receive until the beginning— we ask for those reports at the beginning of August, and they must appear publicly by October 1, that's a requirement. There's no way you can get past that date. And they'll be on our website, for example, they'll be on the schools' websites by October 1.

So many of the actions that were talked about had not yet been reported simply because they weren't due to be reported. You do your reporting on a calendar year.

Senator SANTORUM. Again, I apologize. Those schools that were cited as having discrepancies, they didn't have those problems a year before?

Mr. BAKER. Again, I'm not sure exactly what specifics you're talking about in the article, but I can tell you what we've done is that—basically, I think the activities you're talking about were for 2005. That will be included in the report they'll file this summer, and our folks will take a look at those reports, in light of what's been written, to see if they comply.

Senator SANTORUM. I understand that. My question is, if they were not properly reported in 2005, based on the system they had in place, it would lead one to believe that this is not a new problem, that this is a problem that existed prior to 2005. My question is: Were there problems prior to 2005 that you were aware of?

12

Mr. BAKER. No.

Senator SANTORUM. Thank you.

Chairman SPECTER. Thank you very much, Senator Santorum.

Thank you, Mr. Baker.

Thank you, Mr. Meehan.

We now move to our next panel, the president of Temple University, president of West Chester, president of Drexel, vice president of University of Pennsylvania, vice president of Villanova, counsel to the president of LaSalle, director of Public Safety from St. Joseph's University, and Daniel Carter, senior vice president, Security On Campus.

Senator SANTORUM. Mr. Chairman, while these distinguished people are coming to the dais I just want to apologize, I'm going to have to leave probably before all of them have testified to go to another appointment, but I want to thank you, again, for the opportunity to be here.

Chairman SPECTER. Senator Santorum, we understand your schedule and we thank you for coming and we understand full well you have a collateral undertaking at the moment. Good luck.

Thank you all for coming.

I want to begin with Mr. Daniel Carter, senior vice president, Security On Campus; Master's degree from the University of Tennessee; has worked on the Clery Act modifications since 1992; member of the United States Department of Education, Negotiated Rulemaking.

Thank you for joining us, Mr. Carter, we look forward to your testimony.

STATEMENT OF S. DANIEL CARTER, SENIOR VICE PRESIDENT, SECURITY ON CAMPUS, INC., KING OF PRUSSIA, PENNSYLVANIA

Mr. CARTER. Senator, thank you for the opportunity to appear here today. I have to correct you, but I don't have a Master's degree. Thank you for the promotion, though.

I am pleased to be here today on behalf of the students and campus crime victims to discuss the current state of compliance with and enforcement of the Federal Jeanne Clery Disclosure of Campus Security Policy and Campus Crime Statistics Act.

There have been significant problems with the implementation of this Act. The U.S. Department of Justice found only about a third of all colleges report their crime statistics in a manner fully consistent with the actual requirements. The lack of clear guidance and the lack of strong enforcement have been two major factors contributing to these ongoing Clery Act violations.

Despite these widespread compliance problems, however, there have been major improvements in recent years. More schools are embracing the Act, and the new Clery Act handbook consolidating more than a dozen sources of guidance has been released by the U.S. Department of Education, giving colleges a clear road map to compliance.

Security On Campus, Inc., offers the following recommendations to help this critical process continue: A single campus security policy compliance office should be established within ED that consolidates all Clery Act and post secondary campus security-related functions; implementation and enforcement of the Clery Act should be conducted jointly by the Department of Education and the Department of Justice; institutions should be required to notify students and employees in their Clery Act annual security reports about how to file a complaint. Currently, unless a student locates SOC from our website, securityoncampus.org, or other materials, they are never informed of what to do if their school is violating the law.

The Clery Act technical assistance authorized by Congress at DOJ for campus violence prevention grant recipients ought to be fully funded $200,000 per fiscal year, and expanded to cover all schools that have Clery obligations. Although SOC is here to serve as a free clearinghouse for Clery Act information, there have been no resources for widespread technical assistance at institutions preserved.

There are also several key compliance problems we would like to bring to your attention. Many colleges continue to improperly report their sexual assault statistics. As noted by the DOJ, only about a third do so. Additionally, not all collect the data from every non-law-enforcement official on campus that they are required to.

The public crime log does not always contain all the information that they are supposed to. Over the years we've seen many schools classify rapes as agency assists or miscellaneous incidents. And the date and time is often omitted from these reports.

Timely warnings are not issued in reporting sexual assault cases. When there is an acquaintance sexual assault on campus, many, if not most, schools feel that a timely warning is not warranted, even if the accused student remains on campus. Research, however, has shown that acquaintance rapists are often just as predatory as their stranger rapist counterparts.

Sexual assault victims don't receive proper notice of disciplinary action taken against their alleged assailants. A recent example comes from Temple University, where a young woman contacted us telling us that her alleged rapist had been allowed back on campus. She didn't know this until she saw him in one of her classes.

The Clery Act requires them to tell her. They didn't, because they sent the notice to her old dorm address after she had withdrawn the prior semester. And when they did give it to her, based on our request, it didn't explain why. This is the kind of thing that revictimizes victims over and over again on our college campuses.

Although not directly a Clery Act issue, there's one additional problem we'd like to draw your attention to. Private colleges and universities which employ sworn police often do not disclose their crime reporting information to the public like their counterparts at public colleges and universities do.

I would like to conclude my comments on a positive note, one that gives me hope that our two decades of hard work in memory of Jeanne Clery are truly beginning to show dividends. In partnership with the DOJ's Office for Victims of Crime and the International Association of Campus Law Enforcement Administrators and other organizations, we are putting together, for the first time, a truly multidisciplinary Clery Act training program, and the first seminar will be here in Philadelphia later this year. And we would like for every school on the panel—this is a collaborative multidisciplinary team—to this training session when we host it later this year.

Thank you for the opportunity to address these critical issues and for your decades of work to keep the students safe on campus.

Senator Specter, you are truly one of my heroes, and it's an honor to be here and I'd be happy to answer any questions you might have.

[The prepared statement of Mr. Carter appears as a submission for the record.]

Chairman SPECTER. Thank you very much, Mr. Carter.

We turn now to Dr. David Adamany, president of Temple University, an extraordinary academic record: Harvard, magna cum laude; Harvard Law; Master's from the University of Wisconsin; Ph.D. from the University of Wisconsin; previously had served as the Dean of Wesleyan; and president of Wayne State University; chief executive officer and administrator at a major gigantic educational institution in this city, takes up most of North Philadelphia now. Soon you'll be meeting Drexel at somewhere around 29th Street and Girard.

Dr. Adamany, the floor is yours for 5 minutes.

STATEMENT OF DAVID ADAMANY, PRESIDENT, TEMPLE UNIVERSITY, PHILADELPHIA, PENNSYLVANIA

Mr. ADAMANY. Thank you very much, Mr. Chairman. I appreciate the opportunity to appear.

As you know, we're in one of the most restricted and difficult areas of Philadelphia, and we think we've made good progress. We believe the Clery Act is helpful to us. It tells us to gather statistics, it requires us to look at those statistics, to distribute them, which we do not only by circulating our report but by providing information on our website that's available to every parent and student. We believe that our efforts to comply with the Clery Act provide us with good internal information.

I think improving the safety environment on campus—and that starts at the top—every single morning I turn on my computer and the very first thing I see is the police report from the previous day, which allows me to ask some questions if I notice patterns developing, or to inquire about a particularly sensitive piece, as those arise.

We do offer extensive training programs for both parents and the students, and we think we reach a great many of them. Whenever there is a condition on the campus that we believe poses a danger for students, we circulate information to more than 60 locations, including the student newspaper, and we put it on the website so the campus community can be informed.

Crime rates in our area are very low. We are helped by Pennsylvania law which authorized our police to take jurisdiction off the edges of the campus for several blocks. We patrol those areas and we not only report crime on the campus, but crime in the neighborhood where we have police jurisdiction.

Furthermore, we are tied into the police network for the city of Philadelphia, and we report crimes that they report that are also in our neighborhood. So we have very effective reporting.

We have an extensive, as I said, programs for students to alert them how to avoid crime and how to be assisted if they are victims of crime.

We are proud of our record, realize we can always do more. Our efforts are extraordinary. We have a police department of 110 sworn police officers, all of whom have been to the Academy, all of whom have arrest powers and are armed. We have an additional 74 security guards in our employ, and 314 contract security guards in dormitories and other locations.

Our area is scanned by 285 closed-circuit security cameras which give us constant oversight of the areas in my protection. We occasionally have a slip-up, one was mentioned a moment ago. Quite frankly, if the worst slip-up we ever have is that we send a notice of rape to a student at her stated address, and it does not catch up with her because she withdraws from school and we have to re-deliver it the next semester because she then re-enrolls, we're not in bad shape. But we do make every effort.

Rape victims and students who assert that they are the victims of rape are immediately offered transport to Temple University's health facilities, where we assist them and provide counseling and their complaint is properly processed.

Let me, however, give this warning. In a rape assertion, as in any other case, the student is entitled to due process under the Constitution. Because we are a public institution, until our judicial body has acted, no student can be found to have committed a rape. We move very rigorously on these cases. We do balance the Constitutional rights of the accused with the urgency and the violation of the victim.

Thank you.

[The prepared statement of Dr. Adamany appears as a submission for the record.]

Chairman SPECTER. Thank you very much, Dr. Adamany.

Our next witness is Dr. Madeleine Wing Adler, president of West Chester University. Another distinguished academic record. Bachelor's from Northwestern; Master's from the University of Wisconsin; Ph.D. from the University of Wisconsin; very extensive activities in Chester County; and named Chester County's 1998 Citizen of the Year.

Thank you for coming in today, Dr. Adler. The floor is yours.

STATEMENT OF MADELEINE WING ADLER, PRESIDENT, WEST CHESTER UNIVERSITY, WEST CHESTER, PENNSYLVANIA

Ms. ADLER. Thank you, Mr. Chairman, and thank you for your interest in enhancing the success of the Clery Act and Campus Crime Reporting Act.

We at West Chester University really welcome the opportunity to offer our perspective on how we might work together to improve reporting and enforcement of the Clery Act.

In crime reporting, the fundamental current challenge is that colleges and universities are not using a consistent format to present their data. As a result, accurate comparisons among the institutions are difficult to obtain and crime reports can often be confusing to the reader, be it parent or student or anyone in the community.

This situation is especially true in cases of State law such as Commonwealth of Pennsylvania S73 which require classifications, definitions and formats that are different from those in the Clery Act.

We offer five recommendations that we feel can address this situation and further advance the value of campus crime reporting. Our first recommendation is to establish a single format for reporting crime statistics. This format, perhaps similar to the one used on the Department of Education website, would be used by all colleges and universities in their published annual crime reports. The standard format would print out easy and accurate comparisons among institutions.

Second, we urge the adding of larceny, generally the most common crime on college campuses, to the reportable crimes under the Clery Act.

Third, it is important to ensure that the Department of Education investigators are thoroughly trained in the intricacies of campus security, so that their advice and decisions are consistent and appropriate to the setting situations. We have been informed by a consultant that this is not always the case.

Fourth, we suggest development of a mechanism for ongoing Department of Education assistance and mutual exchange of ideas. You heard about the handbook for campus crime reporting, and it is a valuable document in clarifying numerous points, but no handbook can anticipate every possible situation. We think it would be useful to have a means of sharing Department of Education responses to the points of confusion or new questions otherwise to them. These responses could, perhaps, be made available to all institutions through an annual newsletter or on their website.

Finally, we suggest periodic required meetings between campus police representatives and Department of Education officials to review legislation and compliance issues, update the handbook on campus crime reporting, and provide training.

We talked in the earlier panel about the training that we do, and we do it on campus, and I think it would be more effective if we could work with the Department of Education and have them more intimately involved in our campuses in these training acts.

So I thank you again for this opportunity to help ensure that campus crime reporting is as useful as possible for everyone concerned, and I welcome questions at the end of this presentation.

[The prepared statement of Dr. Adler appears as a submission for the record.]

Chairman SPECTER. Thank you very much, Dr. Adler.

Our next witness is Dr. Constantine Papadakis, president of Drexel University from 1995 to the present. There has been enormous expansion of Drexel during Dr. Papadakis' tenure, taking over the hospital, a great community service, now has a law school and is expanding tremendously. He has a background in education and civil engineering, a Master of Science from the University of Cincinnati; Ph.D. from the University of Michigan.

He has a distinguished academic record administratively. He was Dean of the University of Cincinnati College of Engineering for a decade, and he was awarded the Knight Cavalier D'Official of the

Order of Merit of the Italian Republic. Not too bad for somebody who comes from Greece.

[Laughter.]

Chairman SPECTER. Dr. Papadakis, thank you for coming in today, and we look forward to your testimony.

STATEMENT OF CONSTANTINE PAPADAKIS, PRESIDENT, DREXEL UNIVERSITY, PHILADELPHIA, PENNSYLVANIA

Mr. PAPADAKIS. Thank you, Mr. Chairman.

I would like to concentrate my comments today on a recent news media article of how colleges and universities in Philadelphia complied with the Clery Act. I know my colleagues at all of greater Philadelphia's colleges and universities join me in saying the safety of our students is of paramount importance to all of us. We want students who choose to enroll in our universities based on informed decisions. My own daughter, Maria, attends Drexel University, and lives on campus, and I do care about her safety.

At Drexel we freely share our campus crimes statistics. In addition to publishing this data in our student newspaper, The Triangle, and on our website, we update the website every 24 hours with Clery data. We also publish an online map that indicates the boundaries of reportable Clery infractions.

One of the challenges, though, of complying with the Clery Act is its lack of specificity in defining the reporting boundaries. It was only in 2005 that the handbook on campus crime reporting was published. This handbook goes a long way with its 200 pages to clarify many of the questions regarding the reporting of criminal incidents. However, the reporting boundaries "within the same regionally contiguous geographic area" as stated in the Clery Act are not well defined.

In addition to the Clery Act, our Commonwealth's colleges and universities are required to comply with the Pennsylvania College and University Security Information Act. The Pennsylvania Act and the Clery Act have different reporting requirements, adding to the complexity and the resources needed to collect and report crime statistics.

For example, under the Pennsylvania Act, all crimes involving the students or university are reported in the university's jurisdiction, which, in our case, we interpret to be the greater Philadelphia area. Any crime involving a Drexel student is reported to the Pennsylvania Act if the crime occurs in greater Philadelphia.

Those differences in reporting requirements help to explain why, for example, in 2004 Drexel University reported four robberies under the Clery Act, and 14 robberies under the Pennsylvania Act, in the same amount of time. Additionally, theft and vandalisms are not reportable offenses under the Clery Act, as you heard from Dr. Adler. However, they are reportable offenses under the Pennsylvania Act.

As a result of the multiplicity of those reporting requirements, Drexel has had to hire additional staff members to track all crime statistics, and we have instituted a three-person panel to determine how each incident needs to be classified under the guidance of each of the Acts.

The disparities in reporting crime statistics to the Clery and the Pennsylvania Act may have led to the media misrepresentation of information regarding Philadelphia universities reporting, including Drexel. Specifically, I'm referring to the January 15, 2006, Philadelphia Inquirer article.

The article fails to address the complexity that the nation's colleges and universities face in complying with the Clery Act. In its January 17, 2006 editorial, "Don't Fudge the Numbers," the Inquirer stated that "Drexel University in its 2004 Clery report noted only two robberies while next-door neighbor, University of Pennsylvania, listed 65," implying that this is unexplainable since Penn has 23,000 students and Drexel has 18,000 students, as listed in a table published by the Inquirer within the January 15 article.

However, the Inquirer failed to note that the size of Drexel's campus in West Philadelphia is 40 acres, compared to Penn's 270 acres. Because of communication problems and other complications, the Inquirer also failed to note that of our 18,000 students, Drexel has only 8,000 students on campus in west Philadelphia.

The Inquirer article also tries to cast doubt regarding the boundaries. The Inquirer found eight robberies of Penn students within two blocks of the Drexel campus. None turned up in the Clery filing, said the Inquirer, "about Drexel." Of course they didn't, because they happened two blocks away from our campus boundary, which is our multiple reporting boundary for the Clery Act. However, Drexel properly reported those incidents in our Pennsylvania Act report.

May I continue?

Chairman SPECTER. You may continue, Dr. Papadakis.

Mr. PAPADAKIS. The Inquirer article further states that, "a Drexel student was accosted by an assailant at 30th and Market Streets, just outside the school's mandatory reporting area of the Clery Act. He was chased a block into the Clery zone, beaten and robbed for $5.00," implying that Drexel wrongly failed to include this incident in its Clery report.

How far do we have to go in reporting each incident to make such a differentiation between where the crime started and where the crime ended if it crosses the Clery boundaries, especially if police crime reports are not readily available to a nonlaw enforcement agency like Drexel University? By the way, this incident was also included in our Pennsylvania Act report.

We want to make certain that there is a clear understanding of the difference between the Clery Act and Pennsylvania Act. We also want to make clear the fact that the Inquirer, in its article and in its editorial, confused the two Acts and the reporting requirements. The universities have not reported yet, as Senator Santorum asked, the 2005 statistics of the Clery Act, which will be reported this coming October.

Thank you.

[The prepared statement of Dr. Papadakis appears as a submission for the record.]

Chairman SPECTER. Thank you very much, Dr. Papadakis.

Our next witness is Maureen Rush, vice president of the division of public safety of the University of Pennsylvania; Master's degree from the University of Pennsylvania School of Arts and Sciences;

has been chief of the University of Pennsylvania Police Department, 1996 to 2000; was a police officer in the city of Philadelphia from 1976 to 1994. One of the first 100 women police officers hired by the City to work street patrol.

You came to the department just a little late, Ms. Rush, to be a district attorney detective in my office. You have quite a record. We look forward to your testimony.

STATEMENT OF MAUREEN S. RUSH, VICE PRESIDENT, DIVISION OF PUBLIC SAFETY, UNIVERSITY OF PENNSYLVANIA, PHILADELPHIA, PENNSYLVANIA

Ms. RUSH. Thank you. Good afternoon, Senator Specter. I was also one of your neighbors, but we won't go there.

On behalf of President Gutmann, she's unable to be here today due to some travel, but she sends her regards. It's my pleasure, on behalf of President Gutmann and the University of Pennsylvania, to speak to you about our standards of crime reporting as they relate to the Clery Act, and to share some of our lessons learned for enhanced Clery compliance.

At Penn we believe that safety and security is a shared responsibility, and that the best protection against crime is an aware and informed and alert community, along with a strong law enforcement presence. As such, we are constantly improving our systems to provide students, faculty and staff with the information they need to make wise decisions for their personal safety.

Safety and security are the highest priorities of this administration at the university, as evidenced by the ample resources that President Gutmann has allocated to my division.

I'd like to give you a brief overview of our operations. We have 175 members within the Division of Public Safety. We deliver a comprehensive public safety program that includes 116-member internationally accredited sworn police department that has full powers of arrest and carries weapons. We have a best-in-class security technology network of 76 Pantec zoom cameras, CCPB cameras, and more than 200 moonlight emergency phones on and off campus. We also contract a security force through Allied Barton Security of over 410 security officers, who supplement the police department on patrol. They also staff our academic and residential buildings.

We also offer an array of educational safety presentations and victim support services, as well as having a fully staffed, 24-hour-a-day emergency communication center that we call our Intercom Center.

It is for these efforts, and particularly our community policing and security technology initiatives, that Penn was awarded the Jeanne Clery Campus Safety Award in 2003 from Security On Campus. We thank you for that.

It is also the solid infrastructure of technology and resources that helps us comply with and at times exceed the Clery requirements.

Communications is the key to our success. Communications with our partners in the Philadelphia Police Department, our students, faculty and staff, and with the broader West Philadelphia community. We believe that the more we know about what is happening on campus and in the community, the more effective we will be in pooling our resources and making the community safer, through giving the timely warnings when a crime occurs.

That's why in addition to collecting crimes reported through our emergency 911 system at Penn, we also collect security information from our security departments at both HUP and Presbyterian Hospitals, as well as entering into a memorandum of understanding with the Philadelphia Police Department, and we actually have their 911 CAD dispatch center comes into our center—as does Temple University—so we know what is going on around the campus area.

To facilitate reporting and establish communication networks that aid us is relaying timely notification, we have assigned our Penn police officers as liaisons to all the college houses and resource centers on campus, as well as several citizen organizations in the community such as Town Watch and other community groups.

We go above and beyond Clery's requirements by making available a crime log capturing all reported crimes within our Penn patrol zone which, Senator, is 38th to 43rd Street, Market to Baltimore. It includes Presbyterian Hospital as well, and all in all it's a two and a half square mile radius of patrol.

We also issue a daily e-mail to senior administrators informing them of any incidents that may have occurred in the last 24 hours. When there's an immediate emergency we notify the community via our campus print and electronic media, our public safety website and an emergency list serve that goes through e-mail.

In recent years we've enlisted the help of a core group of student leaders who assist us in disseminating our messages and establishing a campus safety and security compliance committee with members from the Division of Public Safety, Office of Institutional Compliance, and the Office of General Counsel. This Committee helps to distribute and ensure the accuracy of all reporting under the Clery Act.

Some suggestions from Penn, we're fortunate that we have the resources that we do, the relationship that we've built with the Philadelphia Police Department. We think it would benefit all universities to establish similar relationships and systems, especially with regards to accessing data through municipal police departments.

But it would also be helpful if the government enacted legislation mandating municipal police departments to report relevant crime statistics to universities. As the president of Drexel University just alluded to, sometimes that doesn't always happen.

For universities residing in states such as Pennsylvania with the two different requirements, state and Federal, it is confusing, as was noted by the president of West Chester.

Adequate software could also ease the burden, and at Penn we're lucky to have a record management system that we finally were able to enact, that's comprised of a dual reporting system. But all to often, vendors will approach universities with products that they say will comply with the Clery Act when, in fact, they cannot. To rectify this, a standard RFP should be made available to all universities to supply vendors that can really, absolutely build a contract and software that will sufficiently comply with the Clery Act.

The creation of discretionary funds to fund these ventures would also be helpful, in that all universities don't have those resources.

Also, better guidance from the Department of Education regarding interpretational issues such as definition of contiguous property, which is a constant concern for all of us in trying to figure out where we should report and not report.

For universities to take advantage, especially of the new collaborative multidisciplinary Clery Act training that is now being sponsored by the Department of Justice's Office of Victims of Crime, OVC, and the Clerys. The first seminar will be held here in Philadelphia in October, and the University of Pennsylvania looks very forward to joining you on that.

In closing, one of the goals with this legislation is to provide an accurate representation of campus safety to all who try to use universities. In order to better facilitate this, you might consider qualifying statistics by adding such things as the size of the area included in the reporting of the population of the community where the school resides.

There is no doubt that as universities have been held increasingly accountable—

Chairman SPECTER. Ms. Rush, how much longer would you like?

Ms. RUSH. This is the last line, sir.

There is no doubt that as universities have been held increasingly accountable by the various iterations of the Clery Act, that the crime prevention programs have benefited from this.

I thank you very much for the opportunity to present this information today. Thank you for your interest.

[The prepared statement of Ms. Rush appears as a submission for the record.]

Chairman SPECTER. Thank you very much, Ms. Rush.

We turn now to Reverend John Stack, vice president for Student Life at Villanova University; a graduate of Villanova; and has been Dean of Students at Villanova.

Thank you very much for coming in today, Reverend Stack, and we look forward to your testimony.

STATEMENT OF REVEREND JOHN STACK, VICE PRESIDENT, STUDENT LIFE, VILLANOVA UNIVERSITY, VILLANOVA, PENNSYLVANIA

Reverend STACK. Thank you, Senator. I appreciate the opportunity to speak on behalf of Villanova about the critical importance of campus safety.

Villanova's interest in campus safety is not limited to the physical safety of members of our community, although physical safety is paramount. As a Catholic and Augustinian institution of higher learning, Villanova seeks to reflect the spirit of St. Augustine by the cultivation of knowledge, by respect for individual differences, and by adherence to the principle of mutual love and respect to animate every aspect of university life. We're always required to say that little bit about St. Augustine whenever testifying.

[Laughter.]

Chairman SPECTER. Sounds good.

Reverend STACK. In honoring our mission, Villanova hopes to render the spirit of the Clery Act. Villanova annually discloses information about campus crime and emergency reporting procedures, our policy for responding to these reports, and the policies designed by the university to encourage the proper reporting of crimes to the appropriate authorities. We include information about the Public Safety Office on campus, such as the degree of this enforcement authority and its relationship with local police. We also include information about access to and security for the facilities on campus, including residence halls, as well as our procedures for monitoring instances of criminal activity at recognized off-campus student organizations and residences. We also advise community members of our policy for enforcing Federal and state drug and alcohol laws.

Villanova's information dissemination is closely tied with Clery Act's primary goal of providing students and their families with accurate campus crime information. Villanova annually compiles statistics of reporting incidences and makes prompt reports of crimes to the university community when there remains an immediate and substantial threat to the safety of students or staff.

All crimes reported to the university's Public Safety Department are also compiled in a log made available on a daily basis to the public. We also provide a description of the many crime prevention programs Villanova makes available to students and staff, and the frequency of our programs.

Although the Clery Act has been effective to some degree in informing students and families about safety, we choose to do more. We have found that many surveys support our experience that students are more and especially responsive to particular safety precautions that tell a story or bring the realities of a failure to use caution home in specific ways.

In a random sampling of students at three different post secondary schools, the number of students reported having read flyers or articles on campus relating to crime and safety equaled 52 percent. And 40 percent of female respondents reportedly made changes to their personal safety plans as a result of this information.

Student response to these more informal and timely approaches to educating members of the campus community were higher than the reported response in the annual crime disclosure information. Students unmoved by a page of statistics with dry, official campus policies might be more motivated to read crime safety tips or attend a self-defense workshop. If the information is provided in a way that encourages students or relates to their daily lives, they may well see the advantage and change their own habits.

For these reasons, Villanova uses many other means to communicate safety issues to our community. Just by way of a few examples, some of the measures we employ include safety tips for academic break period safety; car safety; sign-up witness; crime reporting capability; information sheets on stalking on campus; use of a sexual assault interventionist; crime awareness games with prizes; published interviews with public safety professionals; self-defense training on campus; and crime awareness sessions with coaches and student athletes.

At Villanova, the safety and welfare of every student is of paramount importance. The organization Security On Campus recently honored Villanova with an award for our accomplishments in the area of campus safety. While it respects the efforts of the Clery family, Security On Campus and other organizations have encouraged college officials nationwide to be vigilant regarding the protection and safety of students.

That being said, there is a challenge that awaits all college administrators, a challenge that lies much deeper than reporting crime statistics. Whether a college or university is located in Center City Philadelphia, the Main Line or the more rural part of the Commonwealth, each campus community is challenged to convince traditional college-aged students that they must take responsibility for at least their own personal safety, and ideally for the safety of their fellow students.

Most traditional college-aged students do not believe that they themselves will be a victim of crime, let alone a violent crime. For example, their willingness to allow a "innocent looking stranger" into a residence hall without asking questions or asking for identification invites a crime to occur.

The Clerys are to be commended for their dedicated efforts that have brought campus safety to the forefront for parents and college administrators. However, crime reporting is not enough. There's a duty of each institution to make concerted efforts to educate its community members about the importance of personal safety.

It's my opinion that no Federal or state legislation can be enacted that will protect students from their own mistakes or the decisions of others to harm another person. The fact that Villanova or any other school is in a safe neighborhood and reports low crime statistics is no guarantee that a serious crime will not occur. By its nature, criminal activity is often random.

Through the efforts of the Clery family, higher educational institutions have become more aware of the role of helping students minimize the chance of poor decisionmaking that might place themselves in danger.

Villanova strives to maintain and improve its record of campus safety in furtherance of its Augustinian mission to live as a community of friends learning together. Students and institutions working together can make the difference in keeping a campus safe.

Thank you for the opportunity today.

[The prepared statement of Rev. Stack appears as a submission for the record.]

Chairman SPECTER. Thank you very much, Reverend Stack.

Our next witness is Mr. Edward Turzanski, counsel to the president and assistant vice president for Government and Community Relations at LaSalle. He's a senior fellow for the Center for Terrorism and Counterterrorism; member of the Coast Guard, Department of Homeland Security; Bachelor's degree from LaSalle; Master's from Villanova; national security seminar, U.S. War College.

Thank you very much for coming in today, Mr. Turzanski, and we look forward to your testimony.

24

STATEMENT OF EDWARD A. TURZANSKI, ESQ., COUNSEL TO THE PRESIDENT OF LASALLE UNIVERSITY, ASSISTANT VICE PRESIDENT FOR GOVERNMENT AND COMMUNITY RELATIONS, PHILADELPHIA, PENNSYLVANIA

Mr. TURZANSKI. Thank you, Mr. Chairman.

In the interest of putting our time to the best productive use, I've entered into the record a statement. I'd like to emphasize one portion of that which may not have been treated in the same measure by my colleagues.

First of all, by means of our educational mission, our religious beliefs, our moral considerations, LaSalle has always placed a high premium on the safety and security of its students and employees. For that reason, we have long had pure education programs for drug and alcohol issues. In fact, we're among a group of about 20 percent of all colleges and universities recognized by the Department of Justice as having these kinds of programs.

We have long had a very good relationship, working relationship with the 14th and 35th Philadelphia Police Departments, very high number of former police officers are in our security force, as well as soon-to-be Philadelphia police officers. So we have a good operational relationship with Philadelphia police.

We've had very effective sexual awareness, victim awareness, drug and alcohol education and awareness programs. And despite this, we welcome the arrival of the Clery Act, because, as has been said by my colleagues and by Mr. Meehan in the panel before us, it gives us an opportunity to use common language for the purposes of sharing best practices.

If there's a lesson to be drawn from LaSalle's experience, it speaks to that article that was in the Philadelphia Inquirer where we were very briefly mentioned, but also by way of criticism, and it had to do with an incident that was—an alleged incident that was brought to our attention in the summer of 2004 concerning alleged sexual assault. That, in turn, brought another individual forward who had alleged a sexual assault from the year 2003.

Immediately we cooperated with the Philadelphia police when we learned of these allegations. They launched their investigations and we launched our own internal investigation.

Faculty, university legal counsel, a nationally known Clery compliance consultant were all brought together for the purposes of looking at what we were doing to see how well we had complied with Clery, specifically to find out what happened in these two particular incidents, and then to see what lessons had to be drawn so that we could make our compliance with Clery better, but also serve the very specific purpose, not just living with the letter of Clery, but specifically with its spirit.

What we found is that we had some very sound procedures in place. In some cases we were even stronger than Clery called for. But we also found room for improvement. I think that's the thrust of what we would like to get across. Despite the fact that we had very good policies and procedures in place for the reporting of crimes, and that we had very effective measures for helping students know what resources were available and we were disseminating information on a realtime and a timely basis, we had an opportunity to look into our procedures and find that we could further enhance dissemination of timely warnings.

We took measures to enhance specialized training on crime classification and report writing so that our student life and our security people were talking about the same things. We also reached out to our counselors and to our religious clergy who, under Clery, were not required to report allegations of sexual assault, and said to them, without violating confidentiality, please let us know, at least let us know that something happened so that we can report this.

We also enhanced programs that we had had in the past in terms of letting students know what was available for victim counseling, as well as enhancing our security perimeter. Our security perimeter, through use of a higher bike patrol, goes well beyond what is required in Clery.

And again, Senator, what we tried to do was to look at what we had in place, and recognizing that we could build on that, to live within the spirit of what Clery called for. We have very high confidence that we did that. And it's our belief that hearings like this work with watchdog groups like Campus Crime, Incorporated. And through collaborative efforts that are warehoused through the Department of Education, we have an opportunity to inform what is the best practice.

Clery is better today than it was at the time of its introduction. So is our compliance. It's our belief that 5 years from now it will be better than it is today, 10 years from now... We have to keep pace with that, and it's our interest to do so.

Thank you, sir.

[The prepared statement of Mr. Turzanski appears as a submission for the record.]

Chairman SPECTER. Thank you. Thank you very much, Mr. Turzanski.

Our final witness is Mr. Bill Mattioli, Director of Public Safety of St. Joseph's University. Like Ms. Rush, Mr. Mattioli has extensive experience on the Philadelphia Police Department, from 1970 to 1996; and as a public safety officer at St. Joseph's University.

Thank you for coming in, Mr. Mattioli, and we look forward to your testimony.

STATEMENT OF BILL MATTIOLI, DIRECTOR OF PUBLIC SAFE-TY, ST. JOSEPH'S UNIVERSITY, PHILADELPHIA, PENNSYL-VANIA

Mr. MATTIOLI. Thank you, Senator, for the opportunity to address this hearing.

I'm here on behalf of Father Timothy Lannon, president of St. Joseph's, who apologizes, but he had a previous engagement.

The safety and well-being of our students is of the utmost importance, and I'm happy for the opportunity to discuss our compliance with the Jeanne Clery Disclosure of Campus Security Policy and Campus Crimes Statistics Act, the Clery Act.

I want to assure all the members of the panel, as well as our students and parents, that St. Joseph's University is committed to and takes very seriously its responsibility to comply with the Clery Act. Further, we at St. Joseph's strongly believe that providing our campus community and prospective students with as much information as possible will empower them to make better decisions where matters of safety are concerned. I'd like to take a minute to address these issues with you.

The Clery Act requires the publication of an annual report disclosing campus security policies in 3 years or other selected crime statistics. St. Joseph's collects this data from all incidents reported to the Office of Public Safety and Security, the Office of Residence Life, other campus security authorities and local police departments.

We publish this report and post it on a publicly accessible website, notify all students and employees individually by electronic mail of the availability of the report on the website or its location in print form. We submit our crime statistics to the Department of Education through its web-based data collection system and notify all prospective students and employees of the content and the availability of the report.

The Act also requires schools to make timely warnings to the campus community when there are crimes that pose an ongoing threat to students and employees. When such crimes occur, St. Joseph's security personnel distribute printed flyers containing as much detail as possible to all on-campus residents. These warnings are also posted on a security website and e-mailed to all employees.

Finally, they are posted on the campus internet, which students must use to access their university e-mail accounts, ensuring that off-campus residents and commuter students also receive notification.

The Clery Act requires each institution with a police or security department to maintain a public crime log. At St. Joseph's, not only is this log maintained and publicly available, it is shared with the student newspaper each week so that the items may be published there.

In order to ensure that the information in the log and in our crime statistics reporting is as complete as possible, we work closely with the two police departments that have jurisdiction over our campus. The Philadelphia Police Department shares its crime log with us each day. Lower Merion Township does so on a weekly basis. This allows incidents that happen off campus to be brought to our attention.

In compiling crime data, St. Joseph's policy is to take a broad view of how we define our campus so that we're reporting more data, not less. This allows our students to have as much information as possible to create greater student awareness.

Also, in addition to the open and public log mandated by Clery, we also maintain an open and public log of off-campus offenses that come to our attention, for the same reason.

Crime is a serious issue for every campus in this country. Last fall, St. Joseph's increased its annual security budget by $145,000 to hire off-duty Philadelphia police officers for extra patrol seven nights a week as opposed to the two that we did before.

We also budgeted an additional $140,000 annually to hire additional university officers for residence hall security. This fall we're going to spend an additional $350,000 to enhance campus lighting and our emergency phone system and increase the number of shuttle buses.

We continue to seek new ways to make St. Joseph's even safer than it is now.

Thank you again for the opportunity to address you. And by sharing this information with each other and discussing how we can improve, we can all work together toward making our campuses more secure.

[The prepared statement of Mr. Mattioli appears as a submission for the record.]

Chairman SPECTER. Thank you very much, Mr. Mattioli.

I'll begin with you, Dr. Adler, to start. The Philadelphia Inquirer led with comments about West Chester University. I'm sure you're familiar with them. They had commented that a single sexual assault in 2003 and 2004 was changed into 14, including 10 in residence halls, and burglaries in those years moved from 2 to 45, once publicity was focused.

Do you think you were unfairly treated by the Inquirer?

Ms. ADLER. No. First of all, the university takes full responsibility for the errors that were made. The university reports, as I indicated in my remarks, statistics, both in accordance with the Pennsylvania Act and the Federal Clery Act, and those definitions are different.

The university used the wrong definitions for those crimes. And when those errors surfaced, the university immediately reviewed everything we had reported for the last 5 years. We brought in a consultant, Clery consultant, to help us go through that data to make sure that we were doing it correctly, and we have corrected all those in a very, very timely fashion.

And now we're undergoing more training for all of our folks that are charged with making those reports. And as I also said in my remarks, I think it would be helpful to all of us to work with the Department of Education to have better training for all of our people to make sure we're doing it.

We regretted that. That was horrifying to me, and we immediately took action to address that.

Chairman SPECTER. Well, you were very direct about it, commendably so. It was a horrifying experience, a pretty substantial wake-up call for your university.

Ms. ADLER. Absolutely.

Chairman SPECTER. Do you think you benefited from that wake-up call in your corrective measures?

Ms. ADLER. No doubt about it. I think we're better than we've ever been. We're committed. I've taken great pride in our Public Safety Department, and particularly on the side—as many have mentioned, on this panel—of our training, work in the residence halls, our work at new student orientation, our work in our weeks of welcome, our work with the community. Our Public Safety Department has been a model for the community. We have— well, the Crisis Response Center for Chester County is located on our campus. Our police officers train, the bike brigades and other police departments and other challenges and communities. So I know that our Public Safety Department works very, very seriously and was as horrified as I was. We jumped immediately to address that. This is not the way we do business.

Chairman SPECTER. Dr. Papadakis, your testimony was a very comprehensive analysis of the Philadelphia Inquirer article.

Do you think Drexel was fairly treated by the article?

Mr. PAPADAKIS. Was not fairly treated, Mr. Chairman.

Chairman SPECTER. Did the impact of the article motivate Drexel to change any of its practices?

Mr. PAPADAKIS. No, Mr. Chairman, we've not.

Actually, if you recognized that the Pennsylvania Act is much more stringent than the Clery Act. If you also appreciate the fact that for the Clery Act of 2004, Drexel reported 66 crime incidents, but for the Pennsylvania Act, Drexel reported 377. We're not afraid to report what happens on our campus or our other campus. We actually had volunteered to consider greater Philadelphia as the place where any of our students—if any of our students has a crime incident, we will report it to the Pennsylvania report.

The fact is that for those 377 incidents reported, theft accounted for 158. And the Clery Act does not provide for theft reports. 100 in the Pennsylvania report were for vandalism, and vandalism is not required to be reported for the Clery Act.

So when the Philadelphia Inquirer says "the best strategy for schools worrying about the competitive world of student improvement is not to hide crime," we think that this implies the university's conceal crimes in order to not lose potential students. That is absolutely untrue for any of us. All of us report about four times or five times more crime incident statistics to Pennsylvania than to the Clery Act.

Chairman SPECTER. Your testimony dealt with, to some significant extent, the question of boundaries. Have you modified the reporting as to the boundaries issue?

Mr. PAPADAKIS. No. We take the boundaries of the university as the boundaries of reporting. The issue here is that if you go away from those boundaries, where do you stop. Is it two blocks away? Is it four blocks away? Is it the whole Powelton Village? Then we take away the responsibility from the police department.

See, when we—you heard all of us say how many cameras do we have. Forty acres of Drexel are covered by 225 cameras. There are 95 emergency phone boxes on campus. The more we do, the less the police department does. So it becomes an unfunded mandate that our universities have to again work with—not that important. I'm talking about the police—right now the Drexel University patrols north of Powelton Street, south of Spring Garden, between 32nd and 36th Street. We patrol 15 city blocks that don't belong to the college.

Chairman SPECTER. Does the Philadelphia Police Department not patrol that area?

Mr. PAPADAKIS. No. We patrol. And we patrol it because otherwise nobody would.

Chairman SPECTER. Do you think the Clery Act is a good act, Dr. Papadakis?

Mr. PAPADAKIS. Excuse me, Mr. Chairman?

Chairman SPECTER. Do you think the Clery Act is a useful Act, a good Act?

Mr. PAPADAKIS. Absolutely. We want the people to be informed. As I said earlier on, my recommendation would be to try to consolidate the Federal requirements and state requirements, then you have one report instead our people working with two reports.

And because our individual school would interpret those crime statistics are not necessarily school or highly paid nor highly educated, the structure should be very distinct and we should be able to tell them exactly what qualifies and what does not qualify, as the example I brought out about the crime that started outside the Clery boundary and ended up inside the Clery boundary. How do you expect our monitor who is interpreting this information to decide? They made a decision.

Now, you may say well, this person or maybe the president should go to prison because this was misinterpreted. But the fact is that the individual made a judgment call, and the judgment call was that this was not reportable because it happened in the train station, outside Drexel.

So, that is the issue with the boundaries and consolidation of state and Federal would made our life much easier, Mr. Chairman, and I think also would take away the question marks that have been raised by the press and also by you and the committee.

Chairman SPECTER. Dr. Papadakis, I don't think anybody wants to send the president to prison. I don't think so. Certainly none of those present here today. Maybe some of those who are absent.

[Laughter.]

Chairman SPECTER. You don't sign the report, do you, Dr. Papadakis, for the Clery Act?

Mr. PAPADAKIS. No, I don't. Because nobody asked me to. Like the Sarbanes-Oxley, chief executives sign the report and take responsibility for it, like financial statements and the surveys. As you probably know, Drexel has volunteered to implement Sarbanes and we're very happy to certify whatever is required of us. But as I said, nobody has asked me to sign a report.

Chairman SPECTER. Dr. Adamany, do you think it would be helpful or appropriate to have the president of the university sign? Dr. Papadakis accurately refers to Sarbanes-Oxley, which is widely criticized by corporate executives as being unduly burdensome. You do administer a big university, in a big part of the city of Philadelphia, so do you think it would be appropriate to ask, or would there be better enforcement if, the president were required to sign it?

Mr. ADAMANY. Quite frankly, Senator, I don't. We're already required to sign certain audit reports, reports to the NCAA.

Anybody who believes that a university president with broad responsibilities is reading through hundreds or thousands of pages of reports that are being filed is really misled. And while I know they all attest that they do it, if you'll forgive me for being just a bit skeptical that the CEOs of large corporations are reading and verifying all of the data.

Chairman SPECTER. You don't think that the CEO would have any more incentives to dig in?

I'll take a 1-minute leave from questioning you to tell you a short story of the autobiography of Charles Evans Hughes, who became Justice of the Supreme Court, later Chief Justice, and ran for President.

He was an insurance investigator for the State of New York shortly after the turn of the 20th century, and he would interview CEOs of insurance companies. And one day he walked into the office of the chief executive officer and the secretary brought a big stack of papers, and one after another the CEO signed them without reading them. Charles Evans Hughes said to the corporate officer, Do you always sign vouchers without reading them? The man said, Hell, I thought those were affidavits.

[Laughter.]

Chairman SPECTER. Ms. Rush and Mr. Mattioli, law enforcement officers, police officers, do you think it would make any difference in compliance if there was, as Dr. Papadakis put it, a jail sentence for the president at the end of the trail as opposed to a fine? Would that improve motivation and deterrence? You two have been experienced in this field.

Ms. RUSH. I would think that that would not be any more a deterrent, but I do think Federal funds to universities being withheld would certainly be a wake-up call for people.

Chairman SPECTER. Tougher to withhold your money than send you to jail?

Ms. RUSH. I think jail would be time off, or a vacation.

[Laughter.]

Chairman SPECTER. In Philadelphia hardly anyone goes to jail anyway, except in the Federal court.

[Laughter.]

Chairman SPECTER. What do you think, Mr. Mattioli?

Mr. MATTIOLI. No, I don't think jail would be necessary either. But with fines, I was surprised to find out there were only three. I've been afraid of the Clery audits for the last 10 years.

Chairman SPECTER. You think now that you know there were only three you won't be so diligent? I think that was a bad statistic to disclose.

[Laughter.]

Chairman SPECTER. Reverend Stack, has the Department of Education ever contacted your university?

Reverend STACK. Not that I'm aware of, with regard to Clery reporting.

Chairman SPECTER. Mr. Turzanski, has the Department of Education, to your knowledge, ever contacted LaSalle?

Mr. TURZANSKI. We're in discussion with the Department over those events that I referenced from 2003–2004.

Chairman SPECTER. Over your reporting of the Clery Act?

Mr. TURZANSKI. It was not reporting with Clery Act, it was sharing information with staff concerning their obligations under Clery. What we had were two coaches who, it was alleged, did not tell an alleged victim where she could go to report a problem she had.

Chairman SPECTER. OK. So that's information. But nobody has ever contacted LaSalle and said "We've taken a look at your report and we think it's insufficient?"

Mr. TURZANSKI. No, sir.

Chairman SPECTER. Has anyone, of any of the educational institutions here, been contacted by the U.S. Department of Education to raise a question about the reporting under the Clery Act?

31

Mr. PAPADAKIS. No. We have actually been contacting them asking questions.

Chairman SPECTER. Mr. Carter, you have something to say, but first I'll ask you a question.

Do you think that it is conceivable that there is adequate enforcement of the Clery Act with only three fines in 20 years?

Mr. CARTER. Three fines are not adequate. Certainly not every school that is found in violation should be fined, but for those 17 where serious violations have warranted a thorough review, fines should have been seriously considered in every single one of those cases and I know they were not.

And I would also recommend that for those serious cases, that's when the Department of Justice should be involved.

Chairman SPECTER. Do you think, Dr. Adamany, that if there was scrutiny, not necessarily at Temple but just broadly, generically, it would doubtless lead to some infractions, you can't run all the universities and colleges in America for 20 years and have only three infractions, that can't be done, and that if tougher enforcement or some enforcement was present and some fines were imposed that there'd be better reporting, more accurate reporting?

Mr. ADAMANY. I think regular review of the reports by the Department, perhaps on a random basis, a rotating basis, and where there is a preliminary finding if the reports are inadequate, a more thorough audit would be very good.

It would be good not only for the institution that was under scrutiny, but because our higher education associations provide us information relatively quickly, that there is a level of scrutiny and I think everybody would pay more attention to this.

I actually favor outside review and auditing of the university, not only in this respect but in many others. It does help us, and even if done only randomly it alerts all of the institutions.

Senator, if I may make one other point about the dysfunction between the two statutes, the Pennsylvania statute—

Chairman SPECTER. Sure. And then I'll come to you, Reverend Stack.

Mr. ADAMANY. In addition to the difference in the reporting requirements, there is a difference in filing dates, and that seems to be totally nonfunctional.

Chairman SPECTER. A difference in what?

Mr. ADAMANY. Filing dates. Because one report may report certain statistics, the other report reports not only different matters but reports a different time period, and it's inevitable that there's going to be public confusion or confusion in the press, because these numbers don't jibe.

So, to any extent that Federal and state regulations can be brought into conformance, that is helpful to all of us.

Chairman SPECTER. Reverend Stack.

Reverend STACK. Senator, I think it might be a mistake to conclude that because there's so few fines that that's a problem. I think that from the time the Clery Act was enacted that initially schools were on their own to try to figure out how to report it accurately, and then as they got feedback over time, those that did, they clarified that. I think that, as Dr. Papadakis said, there were differences of opinion in terms of the judgment about how to interpret certain things in the Clery Act.

I believe that the information that was published in 2005 that really more clearly does identify, maybe takes away some of the gray areas in interpreting the Act, will lead to a more uniform reporting over time.

It's a shame it took as long as it did to get to that point. I think that's going to make a difference.

Chairman SPECTER. Well, I think that there's no doubt that there's a lot of confusion, a lot of areas of misunderstanding, and nobody wants to fine anybody for that. But there have to be, in this magnitude, this universe of reporting, some serious violations, and enforcement is designed to help the universities do their job and to keep people on their toes, and people respond.

Dr. Adler, do you think the Inquirer article—and I'll ask you, Dr. Papadakis, and I expect two different answers—do you think the Inquirer article was useful in alerting people and putting people a little more on their toes?

Ms. ADLER. I think that it is and I think it alerted us even though, generally speaking, our crime statistics are very, very low, it alerted us to be more conscious of what we needed to do, and I agree that there needs to be more—that I would welcome further study of us on that, but at the same time, I think it has to come with help from the Department of Education to help clarify definitions and to help train our people, as Dr. Papadakis said, in responding to that. Couple that with greater enforcement I think would make the Clery Act a much more powerful tool for us.

Chairman SPECTER. Let me ask for a show of hands of those of you who thought the Inquirer article was helpful.

[All panel members raised hands.]

Chairman SPECTER. Well, that's a fairly good consensus. I'm sure that will lead the Philadelphia Inquirer article tomorrow. If there is a Philadelphia Inquirer article.

[Laughter.]

Mr. PAPADAKIS. It's doubtful that the journalist should delve into this subject in more depth so they understood better the communications and differences between the two Acts and—despite the fact that all of us agreed that the article was helpful in bringing out a subject that some of our citizens in Philadelphia don't probably know about this. Not everybody in the United States knows what the Clery Act is. So bringing awareness, I'll agree that the article was worthwhile. But trying to be sensational, it was not.

Chairman SPECTER. Well, I know what you mean, Dr. Papadakis. There was once a newspaper article about me that could have been more carefully researched. But it wasn't by the Philadelphia Inquirer or any Pennsylvania newspaper.

[Laughter.]

Chairman SPECTER. Anybody else want to make a concluding comment?

Ms. RUSH. Mr. Chairman, I'd just like to go back to the educational component. Steve Heeley is in the audience, and he is the incoming president of the IACLEA, International Association of Campus Law Enforcement Administrators, Daniel Carter, Security On Campus, all come to our conferences, and I've been with campus law enforcement for 11 years, and that whole time every conference this issue has been—the room is standing room only. These people are thirsty for information on how to interpret the DOE regulations.

We've gotten, over the years, the Dear Colleague letters but, again, it wasn't until 2005 that we had the extensive booklet. So, again, was it a mistake at hand or a mistake at heart? I think there are some outliers out there who maybe are purposely trying to withhold information, but I think they're few and far between. I think the real issue is we all strive to get it right and it's difficult sometimes to—you know, contiguous, noncontiguous, the public property, there's so many categories and it changes every year.

So I think having a lot more education, having the Clerys put this program on in October is a great start and more and more continuing education would be really helpful.

Chairman SPECTER. Concluding statement, Dr. Adamany.

Mr. ADAMANY. Yes. Thank you. Senator, I want to thank you for holding the hearings. I think all of us want to do better. My day starts on a high note when I turn on that computer and there is no crime reported on my campus. Every one of us wishes for the welfare and safety of every one of the young people entrusted to us.

By holding these hearings raises public information, raises awareness and raises awareness on the campuses and gives us a chance to suggest ways for this process to improve.

I'd like to thank you on behalf of all the members, thank you for holding the hearings and keeping this issue alive.

Chairman SPECTER. I appreciate your comment.

Mr. CARTER.

Mr. CARTER. Sir, if I could just make a few brief concluding comments.

Unfortunately, for 15 years in many respects the Clery Act has been a toothless tiger. There's been not enough adequate enforcement, and that has got to change. On the other side, we've also got to do a better job of educating schools, as with your help we've been able to do, and we're going to continue to do that.

I've seen two things I take away from the panel today. We need to do a better job of involving more people in this campus policing and security issue. I heard several references to conferences for campus police, references to how the police are handing this. Campus crime in the Clery Act is not just a campus police or security matter. Everyone from the president on down, especially people at the level of vice president of Student Affairs, need to be actively involved in the Clery Act.

We need to enhance understanding of how victims of crime should be treated. The comment that I heard earlier today about we're doing well if we just misplaced a piece of paper, that doesn't cut it. And that victim is in the audience today and I could tell she was upset by that.

Thank you.

Chairman SPECTER. Thank you all for coming today and thank you, more fundamentally, for the jobs you are doing in your colleges and universities. You're doing a great educational service.

And I want to thank the Constitution Center and President Rich Stengel and Joan Specter for opening their facilities to us today.

And I want to thank Connie Clery and Benjamin Clery and the Clery family for what they have done, and the tragedy from Jeanne Clery's brutal rape and murder, I think, has produced awareness on a very critical issue.

And there are some good suggestions, we're going to take a look, maybe we ought to include theft or maybe vandalism as well. Maybe we ought to see if there could be some standardization. That's kind of hard to do with the Federal Government, all 50 states in conformity, but it would certainly ease the administrative burden, which you have plenty of, beyond any question.

But I think this is constructive and I think the Inquirer article was helpful, it's a wake-up call. Not perfect, but the U.S. Senate certainly isn't.

That concludes our hearing.

[Whereupon, at 3:56 p.m., the Committee was adjourned.]

[Submissions for the record follow.]

[Additional material is being retained in the Committee files.]

SUBMISSIONS FOR THE RECORD

STATEMENT OF DR. DAVID ADAMANY
TO THE
UNITED STATES SENATE COMMITTEE ON THE JUDICIARY

Mr. Chairman and members of the Committee, my name is David Adamany and I am the President of Temple University in Philadelphia. I appreciate the opportunity to speak to the Committee today concerning "The Clery Act" and the public safety initiatives underway at Temple.

As the nation's 26th largest institution of higher learning, with over 34,000 students and more than 5,500 full-time faculty and staff members, Temple takes seriously its responsibility to provide a safe and secure learning and work environment. Day-to-day responsibility for our public safety programs rests with the Department of Campus Safety Services. Campus Safety has a broad mission that includes the prevention and investigation of criminal activity on our campuses as well as the creation and administration of programs designed to educate members of our community about personal safety and responsibility.

Temple's campus safety initiatives begin with the Temple University Police Department. The Police Department consists of 111 sworn police professionals—all of whom receive state-mandated police recruit training and have full law enforcement powers. The Police Department is augmented and assisted by a security force of 74 Temple-employed security guards, an additional 314 contract security guards, and a technologic infrastructure that includes 285 closed-circuit security cameras, a network of "Code Blue" emergency telephones, and a 24/7 communications center that is fully integrated with the City of Philadelphia's 9-1-1 system.

In addition to providing patrol, response, and investigation services to the University community, Campus Safety Services sponsors a wide array of educational and outreach events of benefit to the Temple community. For instance, Campus Safety holds safety seminars for new students and employees and sponsors rape-aggression-defense ("RAD") and martial arts classes. Other popular outreach events are our "listening circles" and "coffee with cops" programs, where Temple community members can meet with Campus Safety Services leadership to discuss concerns and make suggestions. Additionally, Campus Safety Services and other University departments have spearheaded a program to install "stadium lights" both on the Temple campus and in the surrounding neighborhood. These lights provide pedestrians with an increased sense of security and are important tools in preventing crime.

With that introduction to campus safety at Temple, let me continue by stating unequivocally that Temple remains strongly committed to its obligations under the Clery Act. In conformance with the Act's requirements, Temple makes a full effort to disclose its current public safety policies and practices to community members, to collect and retain records related to crimes that occur on our campuses, and to disseminate information that enables members of our community to make informed decisions about their safety.

We work to fully disclose our policies and practices in a number of ways. Campus Safety Services' annual report provides information on procedures for students to report criminal actions or emergencies, discusses security of and access to campus facilities, describes the law enforcement authority and jurisdiction of the Temple Police, and details our policies relating to crime prevention, alcohol, illegal drugs, weapons, and sexual assault. This information is also available via Campus Safety Services' website. Students and employees can also contact the Temple Police with questions or concerns at any time, day or night, by dialing either their emergency phone number or their confidential tip line. Temple Police have also created a Special Services Unit to assist victims and address crime prevention issues.

Another way we disclose our policies is by asking Temple police officers to speak on public safety topics at new student orientation sessions in the spring and fall semesters and at the faculty and staff new employee orientations that are held monthly. Temple Police also hold special sessions with Resident Assistants and other residence hall staff to provide these campus leaders with information they can use in their interactions with students. An example of the public safety messages delivered in orientations sessions is Temple Police's new safety campaign entitled "Walk. Don't Talk." Through this program, Temple Police are continually reminding students and employees to be aware of their surroundings and to not become distracted and a target for crime when using cellular telephones, I-Pods and electronic devices in public settings.

Moving from disclosure to records management, Temple collects and retains all records required under the Clery Act. To comply with this provision of the law, we make a written record of all crimes reported to Temple Police and keep a daily crime log that is open for public inspection. We also make an effort to obtain required crime statistics from the Philadelphia Police Department and from other law enforcement agencies with jurisdiction over Temple's campuses. Our close relationship with the Philadelphia Police has enabled us to receive City crime logs electronically on a daily basis and to attend weekly Compstat meetings to discuss crime, patterns, and new initiatives. Temple also notifies pertinent Philadelphia Police Department districts and units of "Part I Crimes" that occur on our campuses for inclusion in the Philadelphia Police Department's statistical reports and for investigative follow-up.

Finally, the Clery Act requires Temple to disseminate crime information to the campus community to enable Temple students, faculty, and staff to make informed decisions about their safety. We satisfy this requirement by providing a timely warning of any crime that may represent an on-going threat to the campus community. Specifically, Temple Police email and fax daily crime logs to approximately sixty locations on campus (including the student newspaper, the Dean of Students, and various administrative and academic offices that interact with students). We also post crime logs and "Owl Alerts" on the Campus Safety website on a daily a basis, distribute our annual report to all students and employees, and provide information on where to obtain information about registered sex offenders.

The Clery Act has served an important role in allowing students and employees, as well as prospective students and their families, to review information about campus safety. With the Committee's permission, I would like to finish this statement by making some suggestions about ways that the Clery Act could be improved to provide more and better information to community members. First, I would recommend that Congress consider adding "theft" to the Clery Act list of reportable offenses. This is the most reported category of crime on university campuses and is not currently covered under the Act. Second, I would recommend that states and the federal government study the issue of combining campus crime acts. For instance, the Pennsylvania Clery Act and the Clery Act require institutions to report different types of crime on different reporting dates. These inconsistencies make compliance difficult.

The Clery Act is a well-intentioned and important law. It should not be, however, the only source of information for students, employees, and other community members. I would strongly encourage all interested persons to visit campuses, to make inquiries, and to gather facts about campus safety. This first-hand experience, along with the publications and data required by the Clery Act, will allow people to make informed decisions about their personal safety.

I hope this statement has shown that campus safety is a partnership that Temple takes very seriously. I am pleased to answer any questions the Committee may have.

CLERY ACT HEARING
Remarks by Madeleine Wing Adler, President
West Chester University of Pennsylvania

Thank you for your interest in enhancing the success of the Clery Act and campus crime reporting. We at West Chester University welcome the opportunity to offer our perspective.

In crime reporting, the fundamental current challenge is that colleges and universities are not using a consistent format to present their data. As a result, accurate comparisons among institutions are difficult to obtain, and crime reports can be confusing to the reader. This situation is especially true in cases where state laws—such as Commonwealth of Pennsylvania Act 73—require classifications, definitions, and formats that are different from those for the Clery Act.

We offer five recommendations that we feel could address this situation and further advance the value of campus crime reporting.

Our first recommendation is to establish a single format for reporting crime statistics. This format—perhaps similar to the one used on the Department of Education Web site—would be used by all colleges and universities in their published annual reports. A single format would permit easy and accurate comparison among institutions.

Second, we urge adding *larceny*—generally the most common crime on college campuses—to the reportable crimes under the Clery Act.

Third, it is important to ensure that Department of Education investigators are thoroughly trained in the intricacies of campus security so that their advice and decisions are consistent and appropriate to the setting and situation.

Fourth, we suggest development of a mechanism for ongoing Department of Education assistance and the mutual exchange of ideas. The *Handbook for Campus Crime Reporting* is valuable in clarifying numerous points, but no handbook can anticipate every possible situation. It would be useful also to have a means of sharing Department of Education responses to the points of confusion or new questions that arise. These responses could perhaps be made available to all institutions through an annual newsletter.

And finally, we suggest periodic required meetings between campus police representatives and Department of Education officials to review legislation and compliance issues, update the *Handbook for Campus Crime Reporting*, and provide training.

Thank you again for this opportunity to help ensure that campus crime reporting is as useful as possible for everyone concerned.

U.S. Department of Education

Statement by Robert Baker, Secretary's Regional Representative, Region III

Senate Judiciary Committee

"Campus Crime: Compliance and Enforcement under the Clery Act."

May 19, 2006

Implementation of the

Jeanne Clery Disclosure of Campus Security Policy and Campus Crime Statistics Act

Mr. Chairman and Members of the Committee:

Thank you for providing me the opportunity to appear before you today to talk about the U.S. Department of Education's implementation of the Jeanne Clery Disclosure of Campus Security Policy and Campus Crime Statistics Act.

Crime on college campuses is frequently in the headlines of the newspapers and lead stories on newscasts and newsmagazines. It is a priority on parents' minds as their children leave home to attend college. We are continuously exposed to examples of what can occur on college campuses and in surrounding communities. This has heightened parents' and students' awareness of these issues. The Department is committed to assisting institutions of higher education in providing students nationwide a safe environment in which to learn and to keeping students, parents, and employees well informed about campus security.

Campus safety is a collaborative effort among various components within institutions of higher education and local law enforcement. The collaboration also extends to the Federal level between the Department of Education and the Department of Justice, including the Federal Bureau of Investigation (FBI) and the United States Attorneys' Offices. In addition, it would be difficult to accomplish our implementation and enforcement efforts without the assistance of groups such as Security On Campus, Inc. (SOC) and the International Association of Campus Law Enforcement Administrators (IACLEA).

Legislative History

A brief overview might help put this issue in perspective. The *Student Right To Know and Campus Security Act* (Public Law 101-542) was signed into law by President George H.W. Bush in 1990 and went into effect on September 1, 1991. Title II of this Act, the *Crime Awareness and Campus Security Act of 1990,* amended the *Higher Education Act of 1965* (HEA) by adding requirements for the collection and reporting of campus crime statistics and information by postsecondary institutions. It requires the disclosure of crime statistics for the most recent three years, as well as disclosure of the institution's current security policies. Institutions are also required to issue timely warnings of campus crimes when necessary. All public and private institutions of higher education participating in the student aid programs under Title IV of the HEA must comply with the requirements of this act. Under the original statutory provisions, campus crime statistics did not have to be reported to the Department, but those statistics are now reported to the Department and made available to the public.

This law was amended when Congress enacted the Campus Sexual Assault
Victim's Bill of Rights as part of the *Higher Education Amendments of 1992* (Public Law
102-325, Section 486(C)), giving victims of sexual assault on campus certain basic rights.
In addition, institutions are required to develop and distribute a policy statement
concerning their campus sexual assault programs targeting the prevention of sex offenses.
This statement must also address the procedures to be followed if a sex offense occurs.

The most recent version of this law was passed as part of the *Higher Education
Amendments Act of 1998* (Section 486(e) of Public Law 105-244). The official title
under this act is the *Jeanne Clery Disclosure of Campus Security Policy and Campus
Crime Statistics Act* (20 U.S.C. 1092(f))(Clery Act). The amendments required the
Department to collect, analyze, and report to Congress information on the incidence of
crime on college campuses. The Department submitted the report to Congress in January
2001. The amendments also expanded the *Student Right to Know and Campus Security
Act of 1990* to include a requirement that all higher education institutions participating in
the Federal student aid programs disclose information regarding the incidence of crimes
on campus in a campus security report available to all students, faculty, staff and, upon
request, prospective students.

The 1998 Amendments made several changes to the disclosure requirements.
Among these changes were the addition of two crimes (arson and negligent
manslaughter) and three types of locations (residence halls, noncampus buildings or
property not geographically contiguous to the campus, and public property immediately
adjacent to a facility that is owned or operated by the institution for education purposes)
that institutions must include in the reported statistics. Institutions that have a campus

police or security department are required to maintain a daily crime log that is available to the public.

The *Clery Act* was further amended in October 2000 by the *Campus Sex Crimes Prevention Act* (Section 1601 of Public Law 106-386). Since 2003, institutions have been required to notify the campus community about where to obtain law enforcement agency information provided by a state concerning registered sex offenders who are on campus.

Policy Guidance and Technical Assistance

On November 1, 1999, the Department published final regulations amending the rules surrounding disclosure of institutional information under the student financial assistance programs authorized under Title IV of the HEA. The regulations were developed through negotiated rulemaking that involved the active participation of program participants and other interested parties such as SOC and IACLEA. These regulations went into effect on July 1, 2000. Since that time, the Department has released Dear Colleague letters, provided other interpretative guidance to institutions, and amended the regulations that govern these requirements.

To help institutions comply with these requirements, the Department, at the direction and urging of Congress, published The Handbook for Campus Crime Reporting in June 2005. The Handbook was developed in response to the needs expressed by the community for more detailed and complete guidance on Clery Act implementation. The Handbook is a compilation of all current departmental guidance and incorporates scenarios, real-life examples, and issues discussed during working group sessions involving representatives from the Department, the FBI, the IACLEA, SOC, and various other stakeholders, including colleges and universities. The <u>Handbook</u> took approximately a year and a half to conceptualize, draft, discuss, review, edit and revise prior to publication. To ensure that the <u>Handbook</u> would meet the needs of all program participants, we held practice training sessions to solicit additional feedback. As a result of that feedback, we made further changes and clarifications in the <u>Handbook</u>. All Title IV campuses were provided copies of the <u>Handbook</u> prior to the start of the 2005 academic year, and it is available free of charge on the Department's website at www.ed.gov/admins/lead/safety/campus.html. The <u>Handbook</u> serves as a valuable resource for institutions in complying with the Clery Act requirements. Prior to its development, there was some confusion in the community with respect to some of the more complex tasks associated with compliance. The <u>Handbook</u> distills policy guidance and reporting requirements into a single, comprehensive, plain language document. Some of the more difficult issues untangled during the creation of the <u>Handbook</u> include property definitions (public property and noncampus properties) and the correct classification of certain crimes (murders, burglaries, and nonforceable sex offenses). Ultimately, with respect to property definitions, we were able to develop definitions that are acceptable and workable for institutions.

Another area of focus for the Department with respect to Clery Act implementation is training. The Department has provided training for institutions, campus security administrators, law enforcement, law enforcement associations, and Department staff. Since 2002, approximately 1000 individuals have participated in our training activities. We continue to get requests for training and invitations to participate in conferences on a weekly basis. We are currently planning a videoconference in conjunction with a regional IACLEA meeting this summer.

As every participating institution knows by now, each year, the Department collects crime statistics from institutions for a three-year period. The data collection cycle runs from late-August through mid-October. We are in the process of sending out notifications to institutions concerning the upcoming August 21-October 13 data collection period. Letters are sent to the Presidents of institutions as well as the campus security survey administrators and include instructions on how to complete the security survey. This survey ultimately provides information to students and their parents on individual institutions and is available directly (at http://ope.ed.gov/security/) as well as through the Department's College Opportunities On-Line website (at http://nces.ed.gov/ipeds/cool/).

Our Campus Security Help Desk for program participants is in its sixth year of operation. Most requests for information are made by phone or e-mail, and we have operators available weekdays from 8 a.m. to 6 p.m. Last year, we received 7,682 phone calls and 1,712 e-mails during the time we were conducting our annual data collection. The topics included requests for Clery Act guidance as well as technical issues concerning use of the web tool. Institutions have quickly learned that anytime they have a reporting question, they can call or e-mail our help desk and we will help them work through the reporting requirements for their particular situation.

We are often asked about the accuracy of the data that institutions report. I wish to stress that although we do not independently audit each submission, our web-based tool contains a number of checks and controls to assist users in reporting accurately. Our

46

web-based tool automatically fills in data from the prior two years based upon an

institution's previous submission. The institution then reports new information for the

third year. The system flags the institution if the data reported for a category is greater or

less than ten percent of the previous year's reporting. These differences alert the Help

Desk to contact the institution to address the apparent discrepancy. Our campus security

Help Desk assists institutions in correctly completing the survey. In fact, they follow up

on any identified internal inconsistencies in data reporting or where there are remarkable

shifts from one year to the next in crimes reported. On completion of the survey, the

institution has to respond to a series of edits before it can lock and submit its data.

Institutions are allowed to correct data from a previous year's submission, but the Help

Desk always follows up with the institution to confirm that the changes are correct.

Department staff also contact an institution anytime a murder or nonforceable sex offense

is reported. We have found that those items are frequently misreported or misclassified.

If an institution questions whether an incident should be reported, we always advise to err

on the side of reporting. We encourage institutions to include a caveat or note on the

report whenever they feel that it is necessary or appropriate. Verification of data

submitted by institutions is very labor-intensive. But we strongly believe that with each

year that passes, the amount and level of discussion taking place between the Department

and institutions during data collection has paid off in terms of better understanding of the

Clery Act requirements. This increased understanding directly translates into improved

compliance and more accurate reporting.

We have achieved great success in our data collection. With the exception of

institutions that were affected by Hurricanes Katrina and Rita last year, we have had a

100 percent response rate in each of the past six years. We are proud of this response rate and believe that it demonstrates a commitment by institutions to comply with the spirit of the Clery Act. It also demonstrates the strength of the Department's determination to ensure compliance with the Act.

Nevertheless, we have identified a few areas in which institutions still need to improve. Larger institutions traditionally have developed a relationship with the local police department, enabling them to easily coordinate crime statistics. However, we see a significant difference in that coordination when it comes to smaller institutions such as proprietary schools, which may, for example, be located in a strip mall. These institutions have had little interaction with the local police. While we have worked to assist these institutions in building relationships with the local police to obtain the data that is needed, this continues to be a source of concern in our data collection process.

Incidence of On-Campus Criminal Offenses

In January 2001, the Department provided a report to Congress entitled The Incidence of Crime on the Campuses of the United States, which described the nature and extent of campus crime. The data in the report covered calendar years 1997, 1998, and 1999. The 1998 Amendments changed the data requirements, so some categories of data were available only for calendar year 1999. Since that time, we have continued to monitor trends in crime on campus by publishing on the Department's website both institutional and summary-level crime statistics. We have not posted these statistics this year because the data for a number of institutions that were affected by the Gulf Coast hurricanes are still unavailable. With that caveat in mind, let me share with you the data we do have for the institutions that did submit crime statistics for 2004. These institutions, which account for more than 99 percent of the institutions of higher education in the United States, reported 45,675 on-campus criminal offenses. Since 2002, the number of on-campus criminal offenses increased by 1.7 percent from 44,928. Between 2003 and 2004, the number of on-campus criminal offenses increased by 1 percent from 45,210. (See Table 1)

Table 1

Summary -- On-Campus Criminal Offenses

	Calendar Year					
			% Change		% Change	
	2002	2003	02->'03	2004	03->'04	02 -> '04
Murder	23	9	-61%	15	66.7%	-35%
Neglient Manslaughter	1	1	0%	0	-100.0%	-100%
Sex Offenses						
Forcible	2,350	2,609	11%	2,649	1.5%	13%
Non-forcible	270	60	-78%	24	-60.0%	-91%
Robbery	2,193	2,123	-3%	2,060	-3.0%	-6%
Aggravated Assault	3,070	3,026	-1%	3,009	-0.6%	-2%
Burglary	29,304	29,689	1%	30,451	2.6%	4%
Motor vehicle theft	6,614	6,650	1%	6,408	-3.6%	-3%
Arson	1,103	1,043	-5%	1,059	1.5%	-4%
Total	44,928	45,210	1%	45,675	1.0%	2%

Of the 45,675 on-campus criminal offenses reported in 2004, two-thirds were burglaries, 14 percent were motor vehicle thefts, 7 percent were aggravated assaults, 6 percent were forcible sex offenses, and 5 percent were robberies (See Chart 1).

On-Campus Criminal Offenses

Chart 1

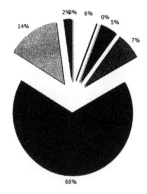

14%   2%0% 6% 0% 5%

7%

- ■ Murder
- ■ Neglient Manslaughter
  Forcible Sex Off
  Non-forcible Sex Off
- ■ Robbery
- ■ Aggravated Assault
- ■ Burglary
- ▨ Motor vehicle theft
- ■ Arson

66%

To put these statistics in perspective, we need to keep in mind what we know from the FBI's Uniform Crime Reporting (UCR) collections. For calendar year 2004, the FBI calculated a violent crime rate – composed of the number of murders, forcible rapes, robbery and aggravated assaults -- of 465 (per 100,000 residents). The rate for on-campus violent criminal offenses was 40 (per 100,000 undergraduate students). In presenting this comparison, it is important that no one misinterprets what we are saying. We are not saying that *any* violent crimes occurring on college campuses should be acceptable. With that, let me turn to a discussion of the Department's efforts to monitor compliance with these requirements.

Monitoring and Enforcement through Program Reviews and Annual Compliance Audits

The Department monitors institutions of postsecondary education that participate in the Federal student aid programs. We currently look at compliance with Clery Act requirements as a part of each and every program review we conduct. The requirements and procedures for these reviews are included in the Program Review Guide. This guide, along with the Handbook I mentioned earlier, is used by our staff every time they visit a campus to conduct an on-site review.

The Department also conducts focused Campus Security program reviews to determine whether an institution is in compliance with the Clery Act. These focused program reviews are initiated based on complaints from a student, campus security official, or institutional official, or information obtained from another program review, or perhaps referral from another office or agency.

Between 1994 and 2006, the Department conducted 4,623 program reviews. Seventeen of those reviews focused on campus security. Of the remaining 4,606 reviews, 252 identified violations of the Clery Act.

From time to time, through these targeted program reviews, we have found significant instances of non-compliance. In these cases, we have imposed fines. In 2000, we imposed a $15,000 fine on Mount St. Clare College. In April 2005, a fine of $200,000 was imposed on Salem International University. Most recently, in October 2005, the Department fined Miami University of Ohio $27,500. We impose fines only when absolutely necessary to ensure continuing compliance with the Clery Act and when evidence points to substantial misrepresentation.

Let me take a minute to describe our approach to a targeted program review. It is important to remember that institutions of postsecondary education vary greatly in terms of type, size, and student population. These differences influence the way our staff prepares to conduct a campus security review.

The first step in the process is to analyze the inquiry and determine whether an on-site program review is appropriate. In some instances, the review team may determine that an off-site focused program review is appropriate. However, before we decide to conduct an off-site review, we must have a high degree of trust in the institution. We might, for example, decide to conduct an off-site review if the institution discovers a campus security matter that may be a violation of the Clery Act, makes a full disclosure, and takes corrective action without prompting or urging by an outside entity. Likewise, if the inquiry deals with a policy interpretation and the institution indicates a willingness to cooperate in whatever manner is necessary to resolve the matter, an off-site review may be appropriate. In most instances, however, it will be necessary to conduct an on-site program review.

If the Department determines an on-site program review is necessary, it must analyze the nature of the complaint and develop a site review plan accordingly. The complaint may be very specific in nature, but it may also be vague and simply refer to general conditions. The site review plan consists of actions that are necessary to resolve the complaint. These actions include interviews with campus security authorities, other institutional staff, and students. Also, Department staff reviews crime statistics, timely warning procedures, annual security reports, judicial procedures, and daily crime logs to ensure that all related records are properly maintained.

We have found several common errors in reporting of campus crimes. For example, certain forcible sex offenses (e.g., incidents of forcible fondling) are misreported as nonforcible sex offenses. Also, when we find an unusually low number of burglaries at a campus with a large residential population, the institution may be miscoding burglaries as 'larcenies', which are not required to be reported under the Clery Act. The review team also notes any sudden increases or decreases in a particular category from one year to the next.

Failure to coordinate information from all relevant sources and to compile, publish, and distribute accurate and complete crime data deprives the campus community, as well as prospective students and their parents, of important safety and security information, and effectively negates the intent of the Clery Act. Such failure may cause readers of the campus security report to have an incomplete perspective on campus security, which may result in persons not taking all necessary steps to provide for their own safety.

On the same note, failure to issue timely warnings of serious and/or on-going threats has the same effect. In all instances of misreporting or failure to comply with the Clery Act, the Department gives explicitly detailed instructions to the institution as to any and all steps needed to bring the institution into compliance.

In addition to program reviews conducted by the Department, every institution that participates in the Federal student aid programs must engage an independent auditor annually to evaluate the institution's compliance with all of the statutory and regulatory requirements. Through this audit resolution process, we resolved 401 violations of the Clery Act between 1994 and 2006.

Conclusion

The fundamental premise of the Clery Act is that having timely and accurate information about the frequency of crimes on college campuses will enable students and prospective students to make good decisions – about where to enroll in college, where to live while at school, and what behavior they will engage in while enrolled. Having complete, accurate, and timely information regarding campus safety is critical as students make these important choices and pay attention to their surroundings and their decisions regarding personal safety while on-campus. The Clery Act has provided students and all members of the campus community access to the critical information they need to make decisions to help ensure their personal safety.

I want to thank the Committee for holding this hearing today on this critical issue and look forward to answering any questions that you have for the Department this afternoon.

Testimony of
S. Daniel Carter, Senior Vice President
Security On Campus, Inc.
Before The United States Senate Committee On The Judiciary
Campus Crime: Compliance And Enforcement Under The Clery Act
May 19, 2006

Good afternoon, Mr. Chairman. I am pleased to be here today on behalf of students and campus crime victims to discuss the current state of compliance with and enforcement of the federal **Jeanne Clery Disclosure of Campus Security Policy and Campus Crime Statistics Act.**

There have been significant problems with the implementation of this Act – the U.S. Department of Justice (DOJ) found that only about a third of all colleges report their crime statistics in a manner fully consistent with the Act's requirements. A lack of clear guidance and a lack of strong enforcement have been two major factors contributing to these Clery Act violations.

Despite these widespread compliance problems, however, there have also been major improvements in recent years. More schools are embracing the Act. And the new Clery Act handbook consolidating more than a dozen sources of guidance has been released by the U.S. Department of Education (ED) giving colleges a clear roadmap to compliance.

Security On Campus, Inc. (SOC) offers the following recommendations to help this critical progress continue:

- **A single Campus Security Policy Compliance Office (CSPCO) should be established within ED that consolidates all Clery Act and postsecondary campus security related functions.** Currently regional offices that have neither the expertise nor resources necessary are solely responsible for implementing and enforcing the Act. No authoritative source for guidance currently exists either.

- **Implementation and enforcement of the Clery Act should be conducted jointly by ED and DOJ.** DOJ possesses significant crime reporting and crime victim assistance expertise that ED lacks. They are also best suited to handle enforcement in cases involving serious violations since ED is primarily a partner rather than a regulator. Nearly 600 schools, out of 6,000, have been found in violation but only 3 have been fined.

- **Institutions should be required to notify students and employees in their Clery Act annual security reports about how they can file a complaint.** Currently unless a student locates SOC through our web site, **securityoncampus.org**, or other materials they are never informed about what to do if their school is violating the law.

- **The Clery Act technical assistance authorized by Congress at DOJ for Campus Violence Prevention Grant recipients ought to be fully funded at $200,000 per fiscal year and expanded to cover all schools that have Clery obligations.** Although SOC has for many years served as a free clearinghouse for Clery Act information there have been no resources for widespread technical assistance to be offered to institutions.

There are also several key compliance problems that we would like to bring to your attention:

- **Many colleges continue to improperly report their sexual assault statistics.** As noted by the DOJ only about a third properly use the inclusive term "forcible sex-offenses" as required by Clery. Additionally not all collect this data from every non law-enforcement official on campus who is supposed to report, such as deans and housing officers. These are not mere technical problems and significantly affect the information students get.

- **The public crime log does not always contain all of the information it is supposed to.** Over the years we've seen many cases of schools classifying crimes as serious as rape as innocuous things like "agency assist" or "miscellaneous." Another very common problem is omission of the actual date and time of the offense, critical to knowing when dangers actually happen.

- **Timely warnings are not issued in acquaintance sexual assault cases.** When there is an acquaintance sexual assault on campus many if not most schools feel that a timely warning is not warranted even if the accused student remains on campus. Research, however, has shown that acquaintance rapists are as predatory as their stranger rapist counterparts. Students ought to be warned about this danger.

- **Sexual assault victims don't receive proper notice of disciplinary action taken against their alleged assailants.** A recent example comes from Temple University where one victim's notice was apparently sent to her old residence hall address instead of her home after she had withdrawn for the semester. This left her unaware that on appeal the accused's expulsion had been reversed until she ended up in a class with her alleged assailant the next semester, a very traumatic experience. Even when we helped her get that notice, four months late, it didn't explain why the expulsion had been reversed.

Although not directly a Clery Act issue there is one additional problem that warrants a serious review. Many private colleges that employ sworn police officers do not allow the public to have the same access to actual crime report information that state law requires of police officers working at public colleges or in local jurisdictions. Colleges in Georgia and Massachusetts even recently won state court rulings that said they didn't have to turn over these records. This denies students at private colleges equal protection under the law putting them at undue risk.

I would like to conclude my comments on a positive note though, one that gives me hope that our two decades of hard work in memory of Jeanne Clery are truly beginning to show dividends. In partnership with DOJ's **Office for Victims of Crime** and organizations like the **International Association of Campus Law Enforcement Administrators** (IACLEA) we are putting together the first ever multi-disciplinary Clery Act training program. It will bring together all of the puzzle pieces needed to comply with the Act. Our first session will be offered right here in Philadelphia later this year. We'd like to invite all area schools to send teams to this event.

Thank you again for this opportunity to address these critical issues, and for your decades of work to keep students safe on campus. I would now be happy to answer any questions.

Clery Act Hearing
Remarks by Bill Mattioli
St. Joseph's University

Thank you very much for the chance to address this hearing. My name is William Mattioli, and I'm the director of public safety and security at Saint Joseph's University. The safety and well being of our students is of the utmost importance, and I'm happy for the opportunity to discuss our compliance with the Jeanne Clery Disclosure of Campus Security Policy and Campus Crime Statistics Act, or Clery Act.

I want to assure all of the members of the panel, as well as all of our students and their parents, that Saint Joseph's University is committed to and takes very seriously its responsibility to comply with the Clery Act. Further, we at Saint Joseph's strongly believe that providing our campus community and prospective students with as much information as possible will empower them to make better decisions where matters of safety are concerned. I'd like to take a minute and address these issues with you.

The Clery Act requires the publication of an annual report disclosing campus security policies and three years worth of selected crime statistics. Saint Joseph's collects this data from all incidents reported to the Office of Public Safety and Security, the Office of Residence Life, other campus security authorities, and local police departments. We publish this report and post it on a publicly accessible Web site, notify all students and employees individually by electronic mail of the availability of the report on the Web site or in print form, submit our crime statistics to the Department of Education through its Web-based data collection system, and notify all prospective students and employees of the content and availability of the report.

The Act also requires schools to make timely warnings to the campus community about crimes that pose an ongoing threat to students and employees. When such crimes occur, Saint Joseph's security personnel distribute printed flyers containing as many details as possible to all on-campus residents. These warnings are also posted on the security Web site and e-mailed to all employees. Finally, they are posted on a campus intranet, which students must use to access their University e-mail accounts, ensuring that off-campus resident and commuter students also receive notification.

The Clery Act requires each institution with a police or security department to maintain a public crime log. At Saint Joseph's, not only is this log maintained and publicly available, it is shared with the student newspaper each week so that items may be published there. In order to ensure that the information in the log and in our crime statistics reporting is as complete as possible, we work very closely with the two police departments that have jurisdiction over our campus. The Philadelphia Police Department shares its crime log with us each day; Lower Merion Township does so on a weekly basis. This allows incidents that happen off campus to be brought to our attention.

In compiling crime data, Saint Joseph's policy is to take a broad view of how we define our campus, so that we're reporting more data, not less. This allows our students to have as much information as possible to create greater student awareness. Also, in addition to the open and public log mandated by Clery, we also maintain an open and public log of off-campus offenses that come to our attention, for the same reason.

Crime is a serious issue for every campus in this country. Last fall Saint Joseph's increased its annual security budget by $145,000 to hire off-duty Philadelphia police officers for extra patrolling seven nights a week, up from two. We also budgeted an additional $140,000 annually to hire additional University officers for residence-hall security. This fall, we will spend an additional $350,000 to enhance campus lighting and our emergency phone system, and to increase the number of shuttle buses. And we continue to seek new ways to make Saint Joseph's even safer than it is now.

Thank you again for the opportunity to address you. By sharing information with each other and discussing how we can improve, we can all work toward making our campuses more secure places.

Clery Act Testimony
Constantine Papadakis, Ph.D.
President, Drexel University
May 19, 2006

Good afternoon, Chairman Specter, Senator Santorum, members of the Committee on the Judiciary of the United States Senate, ladies and gentlemen. On behalf of Drexel University, I would like to thank you for holding this Senate Hearing to address campus crime, and for providing Drexel University with a forum to discuss our experience with regard to compliance and enforcement topics of the Clery Act.

For the record, my name is Constantine Papadakis, President of Drexel University, and I hereby submit the following statement as Drexel University's testimony pertaining to the Committee's interest in *Campus Crime: Compliance and Enforcement under the Clery Act.*

It is my understanding that the committee chose to hold this hearing in response to recent news media portrayals of how colleges and universities comply with the Clery Act.

I know my colleagues at all of Greater Philadelphia's colleges and universities join me in saying that the safety of our students is of paramount importance to us. We want students to choose to enroll in our universities based on informed decisions. This is why we are pleased to support the intentions of the Clery Act, and why we adhere to its guidelines. The rationale behind the Clery Act is sound — to make sure that students and their parents are informed about all aspects of campus life when choosing a college.

At Drexel, we freely share our campus crime statistics. In addition to providing the data in our student newspaper *The Triangle* and on a Web site that is updated every 24 hours, we also publish an online map that indicates the boundaries of reportable Clery infractions.

One of the challenges of complying with the Clery Act is its lack of specificity in defining the reporting boundaries. The Act was passed into law in 1990, but it wasn't until 2005 — 15 years later — that the *Handbook for Campus Crime Reporting* was published. While this handbook goes a long way in its 200 pages to clarify many of the questions regarding the reporting of criminal incidents, academic institutions would benefit from a more explicit definition of the required reporting boundaries "within the same reasonably contiguous geographic area" as stated in the Clery Act.

In addition to the Clery Act, our Commonwealth's colleges and universities are required to comply with the Pennsylvania College and University Security Information Act. The Pennsylvania Act and the Clery Act have different reporting requirements, adding to the complexity and resources needed to collect and report crime statistics. For example, under the Pennsylvania College and University Security Information Act all crimes involving the students of a university are reported in the university's jurisdiction, which in our case we interpret to be the Greater Philadelphia area. Also under the Pennsylvania

1

College and University Security Information Act, incidents of crime involving students are reportable in January for the preceding year, while the Clery Act does not require that crime statistics be reported until October for the preceding year. These differences in reporting requirements help to explain why, in 2004, Drexel University reported four robberies under the Clery Act and 14 under the Pennsylvania College and University Security Information Act. Additionally, theft and vandalism are not reportable offenses under the Clery Act. However, they are reportable offenses under the Pennsylvania College and University Security Information Act. As a result of the multiplicity of reporting requirements, Drexel has had to hire a staff member to track all crime statistics and use a three-person panel to determine how each incident needs to be classified under the guidelines of each Act.

The disparities in reporting crime statistics through the Clery and Pennsylvania Acts may have led to the media's misrepresentation of information regarding Drexel's, as well as other Philadelphia colleges' and universities' efforts to process, collect, analyze and report crime statistics to the United States Department of Education.

Specifically, I am referring to the January 15, 2006 *Philadelphia Inquirer* article titled *On Campus, creating an illusion by crime data – many schools paint a misleading picture by how they report crime- or fail to*. I believe that the article fails to address the complexity that the nation's colleges and universities face in complying with the Clery Act. In its January 17, 2006 editorial, *Don't Fudge the Numbers*, the *Inquirer* stated that "Drexel University, in its 2004 Clery report, noted only two robberies, while next-door neighbor University of Pennsylvania listed 65," implying that this discrepancy was unexplainable since Penn has 23,305 students and Drexel, 17,656, as listed in a table published by the *Inquirer* with the January 15 article. However, the *Inquirer* failed to note that Drexel's campus in West Philadelphia is 40 acres compared to Penn's 270 acres and that because of our cooperative education program, part-time programs and our other campus locations, of Drexel's 17,656 students, fewer than 8,000 are on our West Philadelphia campus.

The *Inquirer* article tries to cast doubt on Drexel's reporting by stating "Drexel hews to far tighter reporting boundaries. The *Inquirer* found eight robberies of at least 10 students within two blocks of the campus. None turned up in the Clery filings." Of course they didn't because they happened two blocks away from our campus boundary, which is our mandatory reporting boundary for the Clery Act. However, Drexel properly reported those incidents in its Pennsylvania College and University Security Information Act report.

The *Inquirer* article further states "a Drexel student was accosted by an assailant at 30th and Market Streets, just outside the school's mandatory reporting area. He was chased a block into the Clery Zone, beaten and robbed of $5," implying that Drexel wrongly failed to include this incident in its Clery report. How far do we go in analyzing each incident to make such determinations, especially if police crime reports are not readily available to a non-law enforcement agency? This incident was also included in our Pennsylvania College and University Security Information Act report.

The *Inquirer* editorial further states that "the best strategy for schools worried about the competitive world of student recruitment isn't to hide crime," implying that universities conceal crime statistics in fear of losing potential students. It would indeed be of interest to quantitatively define through national surveys and focus groups what percentage of the 2.4 million college-bound high school seniors study the Clery Act reports of the universities they apply to and what percentage of them say that this was a factor in their decision whether or not to apply.

Efforts to improve the way campus crime statistics are reported to the public, the active interest that the news media has taken in printing articles and televising reports of incidents and help from the government to simplify and clarify the methodology of disclosing crime are all commendable. However, academic institutions should not only focus on reporting crime but should also strive to be proactive in preventing it. Drexel, for example, is using technology developed by our faculty members in a wireless information-exchange platform that allows our public safety officers to command, communicate and adapt tactical plans in routine or emergency situations securely and rapidly.

While the campus crime reporting process continues to improve, there is still more work to be done. Reporters can fact check to ensure the statistics they are disclosing are correctly interpreted. The federal and state governments can adopt laws that will make the reporting process easier and eliminate duplication. A specific standardized definition of campus boundaries needs to be established and adequate access to local police crime reports should be given to academic institutions. Colleges and universities can continue upgrading their public safety departments and continue to comply with the requirements of current laws. Working together, we can make the system better.

Testimony for Senate Hearing
Campus Crime: Compliance and Enforcement under the Clery Act
Friday, May 19, 2006
National Constitution Center
2:00 pm – 4:00 pm

Good afternoon Chairman Specter, Senator Santorum, and other members of the Committee.

President Gutmann regrets she could not be here today due to a previously scheduled engagement that could not be changed. It is my honor to speak on her behalf about our experience with the Jeanne Clery Disclosure of Campus Security Policy and Campus Crime Statistics Act and share some of our "lessons learned" for enhanced Clery compliance.

At Penn, we believe that safety and security is a shared responsibility between public safety officials and the community we serve and as such do everything in our power to provide students, faculty and staff with the information they need to made wise decisions for their personal safety.

At Penn, the safety and security of our students, faculty and staff is our highest priority. The Board of Trustees and President Amy Gutmann have allocated ample resources towards this end as our University continues to expand and engage our West Philadelphia neighbors in collaborations that will advance the Penn Compact of global and local engagement, increased access, and integrated knowledge.

Twenty-four hours a day, 365 days a year the dedicated 175 members Division of Public Safety strive to deliver a comprehensive and integrated safety and security program that includes a 116 member internationally accredited, sworn police force; a best-in-class security technology network of 76 pan tilt zoom CCTV cameras and more than 200 blue light emergency telephones; a contracted force of over 410 security officers who supplement the Penn police on patrol and staff Penn's academic and residential buildings; an array of educational safety presentations and victims' support services; and our emergency communications call center, PennComm.

It was for these efforts – in particular our community policing and security technology initiatives- that the University of Pennsylvania was awarded the Jeanne Clery Campus Safety Award in 2003 by Security of Campus, Inc. It is also this solid infrastructure of technological and human resources that helps us to comply with and at times exceed Clery requirements.

In addition to crimes reported directly to the Division of Public Safety through our emergency 5-1-1 phone system, we take crime reports directly from the field and from separate security departments at both the Hospital of the University of Pennsylvania and Presbyterian Hospital. We also collect data from the City's Computer Aided Dispatch (9-1-1) system. Access to this system allows us to perform a daily audit and reconciliation process on all crime reported, which not only facilitates accuracy in reporting but allows us to generate crime maps that reveal crime trends in our patrol area, as well as the buffer zone surrounding Penn's campus, and assist our police commanders in deploying our resources accordingly.

Accessing data that is reported directly to municipal police departments is a major obstacle for some Universities. Fortunately, we have spent many years nurturing and cultivating our partnership with the Philadelphia Police Department and are fortunate to have the technological capabilities and appropriate agreements in place to gather a complete representation of data.

It would benefit all Universities to establish similar relationships and systems with municipal police departments to facilitate compliance. To assist with this process, it might be helpful to enact legislation mandating municipal police departments report relevant crime statistics to Universities.

Collecting data from non-police sources is itself a formidable task for Universities. To accomplish this, the University of Pennsylvania established a Campus Safety and Security Compliance Committee comprised of members from the Division of Public Safety, Office of Institutional Compliance, and the Office of General Counsel.

This committee was charged with developing procedures to facilitate the creation and distribution of an accurate Annual Campus Safety report. The Committee collaborates with the Facilities and Real Estate Division at Penn to maintain an accurate database of Penn-owned properties, and coordinating outreach to approximately 80 University officials determined to have reporting obligations under the Clery Act.

Each spring, the University's Compliance Officer who is a member of the Committee, distributes a document that details Clery reporting requirements, along with the University of Pennsylvania Crime Statistics Reporting data form to all internal non-police sources.

Persons with interpretational or operational questions are directed to the Division of Public Safety's Special Services Department, which offers Clery reporting training and education.

The Clery Act has been amended three times since its introduction in 1990 (1992, 1998, 2000), and with each iteration the onus was placed on campus administrators to educate themselves about the nuances of the new requirements. The most sweeping changes to the Clery Act were made in 1998 with the expansion of geographic categories, the addition of new crime categories, and the requirement to report disciplinary referrals for alcohol, drug and weapons violations when in the past only arrests for these violations was required.

To eliminate confusion and ensure compliance, the University of Pennsylvania Campus Safety and Security Compliance Committee confers internally regarding any Clery reporting questions and if appropriate consults with the Department of Education or professional organizations such as IACLEA (International Association of Campus Law Enforcement Administrators) and Security on Campus, Inc.

We've found it particularly challenging to comply with both the Clery (federal) and state of Pennsylvania reporting requirements. While our state and federal crime reporting requirements overlap in some regard, there are cases where the crime classification differs between them. The time consuming process of reporting on two different sets of requirements could be alleviated with the help of state or federal grants to fund manpower and/or technologies to fulfill different reporting requirements.

Adequate software can also ease this burden, but too often vendors claim that their product can facilitate Clery reporting without truly understanding the nuances of the Act. To rectify this, a standard RFP should be made available to Universities to supply to vendors bidding for contracts on software that would sufficiently meet the requirements of Clery reporting, and discretionary grants should be made available to Universities to fund this effort.

As an added service to our community, we make available a 60-day crime log capturing all reported crimes within our PENN Patrol Zone- 30th and Market on the East, to 4300 Market on the West, and from Market Street South to Baltimore Avenue, including Presbyterian Hospital- a 2 and 1/5 square mile radius. We post this information electronically (via a kiosk in our main lobby) and make all information available to the public in written format upon request. Also, we email a morning report of all incidents that occurred within the last 24 hours to senior administrators each day.

Key among the Clery Act requirements is the issuance of a "timely warning" when there is an ongoing threat to campus safety. At Penn, in addition to our campus print and electronic media and public website, we employ an Emergency Notification list serve to notify the community of immediate emergencies. When the situation warrants it, the Division of Public Safety will work through University Communications to contact external media.

We've also enlisted student leaders as partners in disseminating our message. The Division of Public Safety recently established a consortium of student leaders who convene on a regular basis to share information and collect feedback on campus safety initiatives. Last semester, this group comprised of the leadership of more than 25 student groups also assisted us in distributing timely information to the student body and was instrumental in encouraging their peers to utilize available safety services, helping to increase use of our walking escort service by more than 200% for the month of December compared to 2004.

Each October, we distribute an electronic and hard copy version of the Annual Security Report to current and prospective students and staff. An electronic version is posted on the DPS website and linked to other sites throughout the University system and an email is sent to all current students with the URL. A hard copy is mailed to each employee and schools are given hard copies of the report to include in their printed recruitment materials. The Division of Human Resources also makes available the same to prospective employees. The University's official journal of record (the Almanac) also prints a full copy of the report.

With the coordination of ample resources and an organizational commitment to transparency, many of the challenges to Clery reporting can be overcome. Since its inception in 1990, the existence of the Clery Act has encouraged Universities to develop systems of accessing and reporting incidents of crime, to build relationships with municipal partners, and become more accessible to consumers of higher education. As Universities are held increasingly accountable, no doubt their crime prevention programs have benefited.

If this legislation is to meet its goal of providing an accurate representation of the campus environment in relation to crime it should include qualifiers for the data that is collected, such as the size of the area included in reporting, along with the population of the city. Additional education and instruction provided to schools by the Department of Education, as well as the creation of new revenue sources to assist reporting agencies in developing technological and organizational tools to enhance compliance, would no doubt increase the Act's effectiveness and continue to make a positive impact on the safety and security of college campuses nationwide.

Submitted by: Maureen S. Rush, M.S., C.P.P., Vice President for Public Safety, University of Pennsylvania

Senate Judiciary Committee Field Hearing
on the Clery Act
National Constitution Center
Philadelphia, Pennsylvania
Friday, 19 May 2006, 2.p.m.
Testimony of
Edward A. Turzanski
Counsel to the President
for Government and Community Relations
La Salle University

Chairman Specter and Senator Santorum, my name is Edward Turzanski and I am Counsel for Government and Community Relations to the President of La Salle University, Brother Michael J. McGinniss. On Behalf of Brother Michael and La Salle, I would like to thank you for allowing us this opportunity to speak to the important issue of understanding and complying with both the letter and spirit of the Clery Act.

As a matter of educational mission and moral imperative, La Salle has always placed a premium on providing its students and employees with a safe learning, working and residential environment. Our security force has always been comprised of a high percentage of former or soon-to-be Philadelphia Police Officers, we have always had a strong working relationship with the 14th and 35th Police Districts (which are contiguous to our campus), and we have always had strict "zero tolerance" alcohol and drug policies.

With this said, the passage of the Clery Act was welcomed by us as a necessary articulation of the kind of student-centered safety ethos that has always characterized La Salle's policies and actions. In addition to giving voice to the critical public good of focusing on the safety and security of students, the Clery Act provides institutions of higher learning with a mechanism by which best practices for the cataloguing and reporting of campus safety and security elements can be shared.

The nature of best practices is driven by continual, critical self-examination and study, which requires patience, intelligence, and a dedication to underlying principle. As an example, the Department of Justice recently reported that only 37% of the nation's colleges and universities have complied with the Clery Act's provisions. Ambiguities in the reporting requirements of the Act and difficulties in classifying certain types of crimes, not defiance of the act, contributed to this somewhat unsettling statistic. The Department of Education's first-time publication of guidance in the Summer of 2005 is a positive step that should help clarify the Clery Act's requirements and thus promote more uniform compliance going forward. Safety-conscious, responsible people of good will do improve upon their efforts. We know this first-hand.

In June, 2004 our University became aware of two alleged incidents which led to an exhaustive self-examination of its policies and practices regarding responses to sexual assault, crime reporting, and Clery Act compliance. An allegation of sexual assault brought to light another alleged sexual assault dating back to 2003. The shock of these allegations, which were antithetical to the moral character of our University, was compounded by allegations that the alleged victim of the 2003 incident had been discouraged from reporting the same.

In addition to providing complete cooperation with the Philadelphia Police in its investigations of the alleged incidents, La Salle immediately began a review of all Clery Act related training, reporting and compliance, with a specific focus on the Athletic Department, as both incidents allegedly involved La Salle athletes and allegations that certain La Salle coaches discouraged, rather than encouraged, the victims of the alleged sexual assaults from reporting the incidents to La Salle Security or to the Philadelphia Police.

The review by La Salle faculty, counsel, and a nationally-known Clery Act expert revealed that while La Salle already had strong policies and practices for crime reporting, sexual assault response and Clery Act compliance – in some instances beyond the standards called for by the Act – there were areas where we could do better with the addition or alteration of policies and training. It is these areas of enhancement of existing policies and procedures that I should like to call your attention.

- We implemented mandatory Clery Act specific training for all Athletic Department staff, including head coaches, assistant coaches and athletic trainers; and we updated Athletic Department manuals and job descriptions to expressly require compliance with both University and federal crime reporting requirements.
- We repeated extensive programming and training for Athletic Department staff and student athletes that had been previously done to emphasize the annual security report and sexual misconduct resource brochures. Among the programs that existed prior to 2004 and which were augmented and repeated were our S.A.V.E. – "Sexual Assault and Violence Ends" series of student-run programs, lectures by outside experts on alcohol and sexual misconduct, sexual harassment training, alcohol and drug education training and character development training. We also re-ran a "Mentors in Violence Prevention" program for all student athletes and Athletic Department Staff which uses hypothetical but common sexual misconduct scenarios to generate discussion and deepen understanding of rights and responsibilities of all involved.
- We enhanced existing Clery Act training, with specific emphasis on crime classification, for Student Affairs and Community Development staff, and we extended the same training to cover academic deans and advisors to student organizations.
- We conducted enhanced incident report writing training, and incident reports were revised to facilitate easier tracking and to allow easier compilation of disciplinary referrals for liquor law, drug law and weapons law violations.
- We revised our policy manuals for Resident Assistants and student organization advisors to emphasize their responsibilities to report all potential crimes.
- We implemented a new policy of requesting that University Counselors and clergy voluntarily report any sexual assaults for inclusion in the publicized crime statistics, even if such reports are made anonymously.

- We further enhanced dissemination of timely warnings by purchasing the "My Team 1" service so that timely warnings could be broadcast to off-campus student phone numbers simultaneously.
- We provided specialized training on crime classification and report writing for our Security Department personnel, and we prepared and disseminated enhanced victim assistance materials.
- We enhanced communication between our Security Department and Student Affairs personnel by stressing a common set of definitions and language to assure accuracy in disciplinary referrals and statistics.
- We extended our safety and security reach even further beyond the area defined by the Clery Act by hiring a contract bicycle security force to supplement existing bicycle patrols outside our campus.
- We held 7 separate training sessions focused entirely on the Clery Act, crime reporting and victim assistance for our faculty and general campus community in 2004-2005, 12 more sessions in 2005-2006, and we will continue to do so annually.
- And we clarified and widely disseminated the four "positions" to whom the campus community is encouraged to report crimes.

Mr. Chairman and members of the committee, before 2004, in print, spoken word, and deed, La Salle stressed drug, alcohol and sexual conduct responsibility; training and awareness of victim support and rights; and practical, prudential education to support healthy life choices for its students. We had very strong sexual assault response policies that were actively disseminated in printed and various electronic forms and through a variety of orientation programs targeted at students, faculty and employees. In fact, according to the Department of Justice, we were among a select group of only 20% of all schools in the country with an active Peer Educator Group which covered the dangers of alcohol and sex as part of our freshman orientation and which reached out to sororities and fraternities in a "Take Back the Night" anti-crime program. It should also be noted that we had, we do, and we will vigorously enforce an alcohol policy at a lower threshold than the law requires, precisely because we want to keep our students safe. Yet after 2004, we found that there was still room to make improvements about which you have just heard.

And it is on this point, Mr. Chairman and members of the Committee, that we would conclude our remarks and ask for your consideration: the Clery Act is better today than when it was first enacted into law, and our compliance with its spirit, which was always faithful, is better in practice today because of our collaboration with our partners in education - the Department of Education - in incorporating the lessons of shared experiences, and because of the inquiries of groups such as "Security on Campus," and this committee La Salle University has and will continue to pledge its every honest effort to build upon and contribute to the body of best practices in educating, informing and keeping safe its students and campus community through the Clery Act.

Thank you.

CPSIA information can be obtained
at www.ICGtesting.com
Printed in the USA
BVHW062045161221
624095BV00005B/60

9 781297 012419